D0484979

Economics of Agricultural Research in Canada

Economics of Agricultural Research in Canada

edited by
K.K. Klein and W.H. Furtan

THE UNIVERSITY OF CALGARY PRESS

ISBN 0-919813-22-4

The University of Calgary Press
2500 University Drive N.W.
Calgary, Alberta, Canada T2N 1N4

Canadian Cataloguing in Publication Data

Main entry under title:
Economics of agricultural research in Canada

Papers presented at a conference held September 1983.
ISBN 0-919813-22-4

1. Agriculture - Research - Economic aspects -
Canada - Congresses. 2. Agriculture - Research -
Canada - Congresses. I. Klein, K. K. (Kurt K.)
II. Furtan, W. H. (W. Hartley)
S542.C3E29 1983   630'.7'2071   C85-091541-4

Cover photo by Barry Service

Printed in Canada

TABLE OF CONTENTS

Introduction. Institutional structures in agricultural research in Canada. Demand relation for commodity specific research. Supply relation of commodity specific research. Allocation relation for commodity specific research. Reduced-form equation. Estimation. Policy implications. Summary.

Introduction. A simple graphical model. A mathematical trade model. Impact on the home country of research and development. Impact on the foreign country of research and development. The case of North American agriculture. Conclusion.

Introduction. Some previous estimates of rates of return. Methodology. An estimate of the benefits to fertilizer producers from adoption of green revolution technology in Indian wheat production. Concluding remarks.

Introduction. Economic framework. Prior analysis of foreign cattle breed project. Posterior analysis of foreign cattle breed project. Discussion.

EMPIRICAL STUDIES ON ECONOMICS AND AGRICULTURAL RESEARCH

Introduction. Procedure for measuring returns to Ontario agricultural research. General assumptions, adjustments and biases. Source of benefits. Benefit spillovers. Second round effects. Investments in Ontario agricultural research and supporting services. Benefits of agricultural research. Input requirement generator model. Constructing fixed technology input-output coefficients. Livestock feed. Limited land and unlimited land analysis. Adjusting labour inputs for increased quality due to higher general education. Calculating the value of inputs saved. Returns to agricultural research and supporting services. Measurement of returns. Sensitivity analysis of returns. Future benefits.

Background. World trade in barley and malting barley. Malting barley. Malt. Beer. Research and exports. Organization of the Canadian malting barley industry. Conceptual model. Research costs. Research returns. Marginal returns. Discussion and scope for further research.

Introduction. Theoretical and methodological considerations. The measurement of social costs. The measurement of social benefits. Aggregate production function shifts attributable to Canadian wheat and rapeseed breeding research. Aggregate production function shifts attributable to all public wheat research in Canada. Results and discussion. The level of social benefits. Social rates of return. Distribution of the social benefits. Summary and concluding comments.

CONTRIBUTORS

GEORGE L. BRINKMAN

Dr. Brinkman is Professor in the School of Agricultural Economics and Extension Education, The University of Guelph. He is currently President of the Canadian Agricultural Economics and Farm Management Society. Professor Brinkman has done extensive research in the areas of value of agricultural research, relationship between farm structure and agricultural productivity, rural development and agricultural policy. He has co-authored two books, including *The Development of Rural America* (1974). Dr. Brinkman has been a consultant to Agriculture Canada and other government agencies.

HARVEY G. BROOKS

Mr. Brooks is an economist in the Pricing and Foreign Competition Division of the Canadian Wheat Board.

COLIN A. CARTER

Dr. Carter is an Assistant Professor in the Department of Agricultural Economics and Farm Management, The University of Manitoba. He has published a number of articles in the area of international trade and welfare economics. He is currently conducting research into the extent of gains and losses to Canadian taxpayers from their expenditures on agricultural research.

W. HARTLEY FURTAN

Dr. Furtan is Head of the Department of Agricultural Economics at The University of Saskatchewan. He has published articles on the economic payoffs to investments in agricultural research in Canada as well as on several related topics. Professor Furtan has recently been a visiting scholar at The University of Chicago.

ARTHUR A. GUITARD

Dr. Guitard was recently President of the Agricultural Institute of Canada. He was previously Director General, Western Region of Agriculture Canada's Research Branch. He has been made an Honourary Life Member of the Canadian Seed Growers Association and a Fellow of the Agricultural Institute of Canada. He has studied and advised on crop production research in the United States, England, France, all of the Scandinavian countries, India, Pakistan, China, Russia and outer Mongolia.

DARRELL L. HUETH

Dr. Hueth is a Professor in the Department of Agricultural and Resource Economics, Oregon State University. He was formerly Chairman of the Department of Resource Economics, The University of Rhode Island. He has been a visiting professor at The University of California, Berkeley. Dr. Hueth has published articles in the fields of applied welfare and natural resource economics. He has co-authored a book, *Applied Welfare Economics and Public Policy*. Professor Hueth has consulted with several organizations including the Environmental Protection Agency and Resources for the Future.

KURT K. KLEIN

Dr. Klein is Associate Professor, Department of Economics, The University of Lethbridge. He was formerly research economist with Agriculture Canada at Lethbridge, Alberta. Dr. Klein has conducted a number of studies on economics of new agricultural technologies in Canada and farm level systems models. He has been a member of several committees investigating agricultural research priorities in western Canada. Dr. Klein has consulted with several government agencies.

BARRY E. PRENTICE

Mr. Prentice is a research associate in the Department of Agricultural Economics and Farm Management, The University of Manitoba. He was formerly employed by the School of Agricultural Economics and Extension Education, University of Guelph.

ANDREW SCHMITZ

Dr. Schmitz, a native of Saskatchewan, is Professor in the Department of Agricultural and Resource Economics, University of California, Berkeley. He has published widely in the areas of welfare economics and international trade. Dr. Schmitz was recently a visiting professor at The University of Saskatchewan.

THEODORE W. SCHULTZ

Dr. Schultz is Charles L. Hutchison Distinguished Service Professor of Economics at The University of Chicago. He was honoured with the Nobel Prize in Economic Science in 1979. He has been made a Fellow of several professional organizations, including the American Farm Economic Association in 1957. He has been a distinguished Fellow of the American Economics Association since 1965. Among his other honours, he has received honourary degrees from several universities. Professor Schultz has devoted much of his long and distinguished professional career to understanding the processes of agricultural development and the special role played by human capital. Among the twenty books he has authored or edited are *Transforming Traditional Agriculture* (1964), *Economic Growth and Agriculture* (1968) and *Investment in Human Capital: The Role of*

Education and of Research (1971). Professor Schultz has been a frequent advisor and consultant to several United States Government and United Nations agencies as well as to many non-profit, private organizations.

ROBERT P. ZENTNER

Dr. Zentner is a research economist with Agriculture Canada in Swift Current, Saskatchewan. He assists biological scientists in planning, designing and conducting their research projects. He has published a number of bioeconomic studies resulting from cooperative research between himself and other scientists.

LIST OF TABLES

LIST OF FIGURES

PREFACE

Agricultural research has contributed indispensably to increasing food output during the past several decades. Living standards have benefited from the availability of more nutritious food, and from the reduced requirement for input resources in food production. Because of this progress, for more than twenty years Canadians have been spending less than 17 percent of their total personal expenditures on the purchase of food.

The technological changes in agriculture did not come easily. Large investments were made in various types of research activities in order to develop today's tecnnology. Further technological change in agriculture will require that society make still more investments.

But, what do we know about the economics of investment in agricultural research in Canada? To which areas should limited research resources be allocated? What have we learned about payoffs to past investment in agricultural research activities in Canada? Is this knowledge useful in planning and conducting future agricultural research? These are some of the key questions that are considered in this book; questions that must be addressed if the limited public funds available are to be effectively used in further research and development.

Papers in this book were presented at a Conference on the Economics of Agricultural Research in Canada, held in Lethbridge, Alberta in September 1983.

Objectives of this book are threefold. The first is to provide a comprehensive description of the Canadian agricultural research establishment and its workings. The second is to outline some of the outstanding theoretical issues facing the agricultural research community in its efforts to obtain public and private sector support for its activities. The third is to provide quantitative evidence of the success of agricultural research in Canada by providing a positive social return on the investment made in it.

The book is planned so that it can be of use to all those involved in Canadian agricultural research, not just agricultural economists. The papers should be of interest to those who teach agricultural science and agricultural economics, especially at the senior undergraduate and graduate levels. Though the mathematical models presented in a few of the papers may be difficult for some readers, the content and conclusions can be understood by all who are concerned with expenditures on agricultural research and development in agriculture. Agricultural economists interested in agricultural research in economies similar to Canada (e.g., United States, New Zealand, Australia, United Kingdom, Western Europe) may also find much of interest in the papers included in this book.

K.K. KLEIN

ACKNOWLEDGEMENTS

The editors gratefully acknowledge the financial support toward publication of this book, and of the Conference upon which this book is based, of the Burns Foods Limited Endowment Fund, the Cleo Mowers Endowment Fund and the Agricultural Institute of Canada. The Conference at which the papers published here were first presented was one of a series of conferences on public policy and management issues sponsored by the School of Management at the University of Lethbridge.

The editors wish to recognize the organizational efforts of Dr. George Lermer, Director, School of Management both for making possible the Conference and realizing the publication of this book.

K.K. KLEIN
W.F. FURTAN

INTRODUCTION

CHAPTER 1

ECONOMICS, RESEARCH AND AGRICULTURE

K. K. Klein

ECONOMIC PAYOFFS TO RESEARCH

Agricultural research activities have been instrumental in generating substantial increases in food output during the past several decades. Living standards, and thus human welfare, have benefited in two major ways from agricultural research: the availability of a greater quantity of the same or more nutritious food, and the requirement for fewer resources in producing food.

Canadian consumers today spend on average only about 17 percent of their personal disposable income on food. This compares to expenditures on food of about 23 percent of total disposable income three decades ago.

As a result of continued investment in agricultural research, fewer resources have been required for the production of this food. Brinkman and Prentice (Chapter 8) estimated that production of the 1978 level of agricultural output in Ontario using early 1950s technology would have cost an extra $2.7 billion. By using more modern methods when they became available rather than relying on early 1950s technology, Ontario farmers achieved a total savings in resource costs during the period 1956-1978 of $46 billion (1978 dollars).

The technological changes which have occurred in agriculture over the past several decades were not free goods. The technology had to be developed. Investments had to be made in various types of research activities. Schultz (Chapter 2) noted that Canada increased *real* expenditures on agricultural research by a factor of 2.3 during the period 1959 to 1980. If more technical change is desired by society, a continuing high level of investment will be required.

Economics researchers have argued that the returns to research are high; they have puzzled over the fact that more generous research budgets have not always been forthcoming. Zentner (Chapter 10) reported average internal rates of return to wheat research in western Canada of more than 30 percent. He also noted that previous research by Nagy and Furtan had estimated the internal rate of return to rapeseed breeding research in western Canada to be over 100 percent. The internal rate of return can be regarded as the compound rate of interest earned on an investment from the date the investment was made. Brinkman and Prentice (Chapter 8) estimated the internal rate of return to all investments in agricultural research in Ontario to be over 65 percent. The benefit-to-cost ratio was 37:1 using a real discount rate of 2 percent and was still over 27:1 for the relatively high real discount rate of 5 percent.

The Brinkman and Prentice study represents an important departure from most empirical investigations of returns to investment on agricultural research in that it includes all research done in a particular geographical area. It is a broadly-based study that does not include just "successful" research on a single commodity. Similar high rates of return to expenditures on agricultural research in other countries are revealed in a summary of twenty-seven studies in the Hueth and Schmitz paper (Chapter 6). These rates of return are certainly much higher than the 10 to 20 percent rates of return expected on many other private and public investments.

In Chapter 6, Hueth and Schmitz explored the possibility that many studies on rates of return to investments in agricultural research may have actually underestimated the true social rate of return. Most economic investigations of research and development in agriculture have analyzed effects only on those who directly produce and consume the commodity; they usually have ignored the effects on indirect participants, specifically the suppliers of inputs. This suggests an important role for joint public and private investments in agricultural research.

Ulrich and Furtan (Chapter 9) reported on a study of jointly funded research on malting barley. In this case public funds were used to develop higher yielding and higher quality varieties of barley. In addition to the public contributions, private industry contributed to research in the malting and brewing areas. The payoff has apparently been high for both participants. The internal rate of return to society was estimated at 50 percent on public expenditures and 74 percent on private expenditures. The private firm also received high returns on this joint investment: 16 percent on public investments in barley breeding and 33 percent on its own investments in research.

The high rates of return to investment in agricultural research that have consistently been shown in Canadian and other studies suggest a major underinvestment by society in this activity. It would seem that a higher level of investment is needed to bring the marginal returns to agricultural research down to levels that approximate those on other types of investments. Furthermore, many of the benefits of agricultural research are distributed in a progressive manner. By reducing the cost of foodstuffs, all consumers of food benefit from the research. And since the poor spend a relatively greater proportion of their income on food purchases than do the wealthy, poor consumers receive a proportionately greater benefit.

It should be noted that not all consumer gains from agricultural research conducted in Canada accrue to Canadian consumers. Zentner (Chapter 10) noted that since a large share of wheat and rapeseed production in Canada is exported, a large share of the consumer benefits from research in these commodities goes to foreign consumers.

In Chapter 5, Carter explored the conditions under which exporting and importing countries gain from agricultural research. He showed mathematically that it was possible for an exporting country to become worse off through agricultural research. The expansion in food production made possible by new technology could make food products relatively cheap and thus alter the relative prices (terms of trade) of a country's imports and exports. This deterioration in an exporting country's terms of trade may outweigh the benefits from an increased production potential in agriculture. However, these detrimental effects apply only to a "large" country, i.e., one that is large enough to have an impact on world prices.

Carter identified areas in agriculture where public expenditures on agricultural research can maximize benefits to the country doing the research (i.e., the home country). These are mostly import competing products like fruits, vegetables and oilseeds. Public research invested on export products should be confined to those that face relatively elastic import demand schedules (i.e., where a small reduction in price will cause imports to increase more than proportionally). Quantities of grain purchased by importing countries have shown little sensitivity to changes in grain prices over the years due primarily to protectionist policies in major importing countries (European Economic Community and Japan). Therefore, it may not be in exporting countries' best interests to continue allocating public funds to research on grain.

AGRICULTURAL RESEARCH IN CANADA

Professional service to the industry of agriculture in Canada began with agricultural research. There has been rapid development of research institutions and programs over the past century.

In the late 1880s it was realized that agricultural production had a base in science, and colleges and faculties of Agriculture came to be established at existing universities or as the first faculties of new universities. All were originally established to teach professionals but soon developed research programs as natural adjuncts to teaching.

In the early years, the Canadian Department of Agriculture (now called Agriculture Canada) and the universities extended research information directly to farmers, mostly in association with their research and teaching. The eastern provinces developed extension services early in the development of the industry and the western provinces developed programs soon after they were created. All provinces had extension programs directed to the producer and supported research as the source of information for their extension programs. Ontario, Quebec and Alberta started their own research programs. Industry has also become involved in supporting research and extension.

From this beginning more than 100 years ago, there has developed in Canada an extensive professional support system for agricultural production. The system consists of education, research and extension activities by universities, provinces, the Federal Government and industry.

The Federal Government is the largest contributor to agricultural research in Canada. The Federal Task Force on Agriculture reported that in 1967, 53 percent of all agricultural research in Canada was sponsored by the Federal Government (p. 397). This compared to 29 percent by universities, 10.6 percent by provincial governments, and 7.4 percent by industry. Brooks and Furtan (Chapter 4) reported that by 1977 the proportion of research effort by each of the major players was: Federal Government 60 percent, universities 28 percent, provincial governments 5 percent and industry 6 percent.

In Chapter 3, Guitard noted that eight faculties and colleges of Agriculture and three faculties and colleges of Veterinary Medicine in Canada provided training in the sciences related to Agriculture. During 1982-83, these institutions had an enrolment of 6,800 undergraduate and 1,670 graduate students. The students were taught by 870 academic staff in the faculties and colleges and by additional staff in related faculties. The operating budget for the faculties and colleges of Agriculture and Veterinary Medicine was approximately $110 million during 1982-83.

During 1982-83 there were approximately 1,800 professionals doing research for agriculture in Canada at a cost of approximately $350 million.

Teaching and research staff still do some extension activities but most of the direct extension is now carried out by staff of provincial departments of agriculture working from strategically located regional and district offices. Based on the number of staff employed by Alberta, Saskatchewan and Ontario, it was estimated that 1,000 professionals are employed in Canada as extension agents and specialists. Using the same base, the annual operating cost of all extension services in Canada was estimated to be $60 million.

Thus, it appears that during 1982-83 some 3,500 professionals were employed to deliver education, research and extension services to the agricultural industry at a cost conservatively estimated at $500 million.

DIRECTION OF AGRICULTURAL RESEARCH

Maximization of social product is frequently suggested as an objective toward which societies strive. Social product can only be maximized, according to Pigou, when the ''marginal social net product'' of each resource is equal in all its uses. Thus, research resources must be allocated in such a way that their marginal social productivity equals the marginal social productivity of all other resources available to society; without that condition being fulfilled, social product cannot be maximized.

Arrow (p. 609) noted that this equality can be ensured by perfect competition in the market place only if:

1) the utility functions of consumers and the transformation functions of producers are well-defined, and

2) the transformation functions do not display indivisibilities.

The first condition implies that there can be no uncertainty in the production and utility relationships. It also implies that all commodities that are relevant either to production or to the welfare of consumers must be traded in the market. Therefore, all property must be private.

These important assumptions of the perfect competition model, i.e., no uncertainty, no indivisibility and appropriable output, cannot often be met in the matter of allocating resources for research activities.

Arrow (p. 616) claimed (and most researchers would undoubtedly agree) that the production of information is an inherently ''risky process, in that the output can never be predicted perfectly from the inputs." Thus, the assumption of perfect knowledge (no uncertainty) cannot be valid.

Indivisibilities in the production side of research are certainly prominent. Most scientists have very specialized training. The ability of a research administrator to substitute among areas of research is usually limited.

Much of the research output (information) cannot be embodied in tradeable goods or services. Tichenor and Ruttan (p. 4) argued that since many of the benefits of research "are not fully appropriable by the firm or individual that incurs the cost of producing them, private profit is an inadequate incentive for production of (this research)."

If a perfectly functioning competitive market cannot provide appropriate price signals for resource allocation to agricultural research, how is the level of funds to agricultural research and the allocation among competing agricultural commodities determined? Brooks and Furtan addressed this question in Chapter 4. This question is of fundamental importance since an understanding of the processes involved will provide insights into the future composition of the agricultural sector and those parts of the industry that can be expected to grow and prosper. Their analysis included institutional as well as economic variables. They concluded that educational levels of farmers and size distribution of farms in a region play an important role in determining the amount and the type of agricultural research that is undertaken.

Schultz (Chapter 2) argued for more decentralized decision making in agricultural research. Competition among researchers and among research institutions can enhance the responsiveness of scientists to changes in economic conditions.

In Canada, the Federal Government uses a very centralized system of control over agricultural research in each of the geographic regions (viz., Maritimes, Quebec, Ontario, Prairies, British Columbia). This ensures no duplication of effort and provides for comprehensive scientific inquiry on most agricultural commodities.

The Research Branch of Agriculture Canada established a "management by objectives" type of program planning structure in 1969. The purpose was to allocate research personnel to projects having specific objectives of achieving stated percentage increases in efficiency, quality and/or production within a given time frame.

Since the inception of the program planning structure, research administrators have experienced difficulty in:

1) establishing realistic goals and objectives,

2) setting priorities on each,

3) measuring the progress of individual research projects in terms which conform to the specified program goals, and

4) evaluating the experimental results in terms of their overall contribution to the development and progress of the agricultural industry.

Setting priorities on individual research projects is important so that limited research funds can be allocated to those projects that have the greatest likelihood of decreasing the real unit costs of production. Allied with the setting of priorities on individual projects is the determination of how best to design and conduct particular research projects, i.e., which breeds or varieties to test, over which set of conditions, for how many years.

In an earlier study Klein developed a systematic procedure to provide information on these problem areas to enhance the probability of correct choices being taken in an ongoing livestock breeding project in Canada. In this study, specific attention was paid to farm level constraints as experienced by farmers in different regions with different resource bases and having different levels of proficiency in various management responsibilities. In Chapter 7 of this volume Klein looks back at the previous study to determine whether or not the recommendations that were made would have been good choices had they been followed. It was concluded that *ex ante* analysis of specific research projects and, in particular, of specific research procedures could be used to advantage in increasing the efficiency of resource use in agricultural research.

CONCLUSION

The studies included in these covers reflect recent discoveries concerning the relative benefits of investing in agricultural research in Canada, as well as indicating considerations for increasing the economic payoff from future agricultural research. As in most areas of scientific inquiry, these studies have only probed the surface of a full understanding of the impacts on Canadian society from investing in agricultural research. They have left a number of questions unanswered. This cross-section of papers is suggestive of the wide and so far unexploited scope of economics research on this topic. It is hoped that this collection of studies will stimulate actions of research administrators to determine the most beneficial methods of allocating their scarce research resources and to document the costs and benefits of their use. By acquiring a full understanding of the economics of research, the best possible case can be made for ensuring continued public support in this high payoff area.

REFERENCES

Arrow, Kenneth J. "Economic Welfare and the Allocation of Resources for Invention." In *The Rate and Direction of Inventive Activity: Economic and Social Factors*. A Report of the National Bureau of Economic Research, New York. Princeton: Princeton University Press, 1962.

Federal Task Force on Agriculture. *Canadian Agriculture in the Seventies*. Ottawa, Canada: Queen's Printer, 1970.

Klein, Kurt K. ''An Investigation into the Evaluation of Applied Research Projects in Agriculture.'' Ph.D. diss., Purdue University, West Lafayette, Indiana, 1976.

Nagy, J.G., and W.H. Furtan. ''Economic Costs and Returns From Crop Development Research: The Case of Rapeseed Breeding in Canada.'' *Canadian Journal of Agricultural Economics* 26 (1978): 1-14.

Pigou, A.C. *The Economics of Welfare*, 4th ed. London: MacMillan and Co. Ltd., 1960.

Tichenor, Phillip J., and Vernon W. Ruttan. ''Problems and Issues.'' In *Resource Allocation for Agricultural Research*, edited by Walter L. Fishel. Minneapolis, Minnesota: University of Minnesota Press, 1971.

CHAPTER 2

AGRICULTURAL RESEARCH: CANADA AND BEYOND

Theodore W. Schultz

Agricultural research is too important to leave to the new breed of reformers to reorganize it. It has become too large to leave it solely to the directors to keep abreast of advances in the sciences and for agricultural scientists to stay on top of changing conditions in agriculture throughout the world. Nor would I argue that economists are up to assessing the real research opportunities.

There are many unsolved problems pertaining to agricultural research. The evidence that is required to clarify the essence of these problems is murky and what needs to be done to improve the efficiency of agricultural research is far from clear. Critical discussion in this symposium should be helpful in clarifying these issues. My purpose is to identify some of the major issues as I see them.

I shall consider the worldwide impressive growth of agricultural research, Borlaug's superb deflator, the remarkable ascent of crop yields, some of the notable agricultural research successes and failures, effects on comparative advantage, flaws in thinking about agriculture and the sciences and, in closing, a little list of additional issues.

GROWTH AND MAGNITUDE OF AGRICULTURAL RESEARCH

In terms of expenditures, agricultural research has become a substantial sector of the economy. We need to ponder the implications of following estimates.[1]

Worldwide expenditures for this purpose in 1980 in U.S. dollars was $7.4 billion. A tidy sum indeed. How much of it is used efficiently?

Twenty-one years ago in 1959, in constant 1980 dollars, expenditures were $2.1 billion. Thus, in real terms, they increased somewhat more than three and one-half times, a remarkable achievement. What explains this high rate of growth?

In the U.S. the corresponding estimates are: for 1959, $564 million and for 1980, $1.1 billion, somewhat less than a twofold real increase in funds. Does this mean that the U.S. agricultural research opportunities were relatively fewer than they were throughout the world?

In Canada, estimates from the same source show $105 million (in U.S. 1980 dollars) and $241 million expenditures in 1980, a 2.3-fold increase. Why did Canada do better on this score than the U.S.?

The U.S.S.R. increased her expenditures for agricultural research from $374 million to $939 million (U.S. 1980 dollars) over this period, a 2.5-fold increase. Did it contribute to the productivity of Soviet agriculture? If not, why not?

The estimate of agricultural scientists' man-years is an alternative measure of the growth and magnitude of agricultural research. In 1980, 148,000 man-years were devoted to this research worldwide.

The U.S. accounted for a little less than 6 percent of this total and Canada for 1.25 percent. These two countries accounted for only 7 percent of world total. Why do we neglect the successes and failures of the 93 percent of these man-years in the rest of the world? Consider the U.S.S.R. once again: it accounted for

21 percent of the total, three times that of Canada and the U.S. combined. What is there to show for it in Soviet agriculture?

NORMAN BORLAUG'S SUPERB DEFLATOR

It is difficult to resist citing his deflator to hold in check our self-acclaimed importance in augmenting the production of food. Whereas Neolithic women invented agriculture and invented many of the food crop species that we have today, our highly skilled plant breeders with all their fancy theories and large expenditures on research have produced only one new food species, *triticale*. Borlaug puts it this way: "The first and greatest green revolution occurred when women decided that something had to be done about their dwindling food supply."[2] Neolithic men, in hunting for meat, were failing to bring home enough to eat. My reading of the research records is that a couple of Canadian agricultural scientists, here in the Prairie Provinces, invented triticale. Three cheers! But why have our many competent plant breeders invented only one? Economists invent new models constantly. You will say, they turn out to be sterile.

INCREASES AND DIFFERENCES IN CROP YIELDS

Since World War II, there has been remarkable progress on two counts; namely, longer life span and higher crop yields. The increases in life span and the reduction of the gap between rich and poor countries are exceedingly important. As of the late 1940s, this gap in life span was large. In general, it has been greatly reduced as a consequence of the marked improvements in health in many low income countries. The welfare implications of the increases in life span in these low income countries is not in doubt despite the fact that they account for most of the observed population growth. The actual declines in fertility are "concealed" by the population growth resulting from increases in life span. Advances in knowledge pertaining to health and increases in the per capita supply of food have both been favourable factors.

The large increase in crop yields is the other major achievement. It has, in large measure, been made possible by the high yielding varieties created by agricultural scientists. The pattern of wheat yields in low income India and high income Canada tell a good bit of the story. Wheat yields during the 1930s were somewhat lower in India than in Canada. By the mid-1940s, yields in Canada were 60 percent higher than in India. Between 1944-46 and 1979-1981, wheat yields in India increased by 131 percent and in Canada by only 16.6 percent. Thus, wheat yields in Canada during 1979-1981 averaged 26.6 bushels and in India, 23.1 bushels per acre, a difference of only 15 percent.

NOTABLE SUCCESSES AND FAILURES

1. The success of most of the International Agricultural Research Centres is not in doubt. There are now thirteen, annual budget about $150 million, supported by thirty-five donors.[3] They have an international dimension that owes

TABLE 1

**COMPARATIVE WHEAT YIELDS
IN CANADA AND INDIA**

Wheat Yields Bushels per Acre

	1930s	1944-46	1979-81
Canada	13	16	26.6
India	11	10	23.1

Source: U.S.D.A. Agricultural Statistics

much to the Rockefeller Foundation and to the pioneering entrepreneurship of the late George Harrar. Frosty Hill, a Canadian, while Vice-President of the Ford Foundation, also was a key research entrepreneur in this innovation.

Successful as these centres have been, I see four limitations: (1) they are not a substitute for ongoing national experiment stations and laboratories in low income countries; (2) the relationship between them and the major research-oriented universities and experiment stations in high income countries is too tenuous; (3) the central management, i.e., the allocation of funds to each of the centres, is becoming over-organized in the sense that too much of the time of the research personnel at the centres is spent on paper work "justifying" research; and, (4) the centre located in Nigeria has concentrated on local food production and it has neglected the important export commodities. More generally, the emphasis that is placed on food production, especially throughout central Africa, has been a serious mistake in view of the fact that the economic comparative advantage was, and continues to be, in the larger gains to be had from the real growth in their exports, primarily of tree crops. Agricultural scientists do not have a sufficient comprehension of the economic importance of the role of comparative advantage in production and trade among nations. There is truth in the dictum, "trade not aid." In fact, agricultural research to promote only food crops in tropical Africa is decidedly harmful to the economy.

2. While India was building her agricultural research capacity, the cultural revolution in China was destroying it in China. The development of the agricultural universities in India is impressive. India now has a core of competent agricultural scientists, with over 2,000 scientist man-years to her credit, and several of her agricultural universities capable of doing respectable graduate training. China is now rebuilding, but it will take at least several decades for China to attain a competent agricultural research capacity on a par with that in place in India.

3. Nigeria was the dominant world exporter of palm tree products. The high yielding variety developed by the long-standing commonwealth experiment station in Nigeria did not replace the low yielding varieties because the high export

tax on palm fruit made it unprofitable to the point that Nigeria has become an importer. What Nigeria destroyed, Malaysia captured. Malaysia is now the dominant world exporter of palm fruit. Producers in Malaysia adopted the high yielding varieties because they were highly profitable as a consequence of the fact that Malaysia approximated a free trade export policy. Economic incentives matter for the contributions of agricultural research to be successful in production.

There are many more successes and failures that are instructive in assessing the factors that determined the various outcomes.

COMPARATIVE ADVANTAGE ALTERED BY AGRICULTURAL RESEARCH

Agricultural production is soil specific, crop and plant specific, animal production specific, market specific and location specific. So are the requirements of agricultural research. Hybrid corn increased the comparative advantage of the heart of the corn belt. Corn production is now much more concentrated in the best parts of the corn belt while other areas have become less important in corn.

In wheat, India's comparative advantage has improved relative to that of Canada. Farmers in India started with 7,400 acres of high yielding wheat in 1965; by 1977, 37 million acres in India were devoted to the new wheat. By 1977, India replaced Canada as the fourth largest producer of wheat; India produced 29 million tons and Canada 19.6 million. In 1965, India imported 376 million bushels of wheat and, in 1977, she exported 17 million bushels.

The comparative advantage of Malaysia has been increased decidedly in both rubber and palm fruit by agricultural research specific to these two crops.

How the gains in productivity alter the comparative advantage of different locations within a country and among countries is not an issue that should burden agricultural scientists. But when agricultural research programs impair the existing comparative advantage of countries as they have in tropical Africa in the case of non-food crops, it is a different matter.

AGRICULTURE AND THE SCIENCES[4]

Read the thirty-five page pronouncement from a mountain in Arkansas, the home of Winrock, with the imprimatur of the Rockefeller Foundation, labeled *Science for Agriculture*, and you will become frustrated unless you have learned to enjoy the logic that Alice in Wonderland faced.

The message is that "Agricultural Science" results in inferior research because it is "a piecemeal approach to gaining crucial, fundamental knowledge...." because it is oriented to agriculture and not to the advancement of the sciences, because there are no established national priorities for agricultural research, and because the U.S. Federal Government has lost control of agricultural research. Bewildered Alice might ask, "Since centrally controlled agriculture is a disaster, would not centrally controlled agricultural research also be a disaster?"

National research priorities are a noble objective. International research priorities would be still nobler. Since the sciences are not country specific and not agriculture specific, why not opt for worldwide science research priorities? Let the United Nations establish them; and, to make sure that the research would be devoted to the established priorities, all research funds would be allocated to an agency designated by the United Nations to assure that it had complete control. Common sense warns us that this would be a nightmare. For the Federal Government to do this for all science research in the U.S. would also be unacceptable, although, according to this report, it is not unthinkable.

The critical flaw of this report is its failure to comprehend the specific nature of the research requirements of agriculture. As already noted, agricultural production is soil specific, crop and plant variety specific, animal production specific, market specific and location specific. Because of all of these specific characteristics, agriculture is by its very nature exceedingly heterogeneous. The research required for the agriculture of California differs greatly from that of Maine. Within most states agriculture is far from homogeneous and so is the required research. To assume that a government agency in Washington, blessed with a highly competent administrator who has at his service the best computer technology, could determine the optimum agricultural research that is required in the United States, is wishful thinking. Priorities and control of agricultural research vested in Washington would be akin to Gosplan. It would be a disaster.

The argument advanced in *Science for Agriculture* is that agricultural research is all too decentralized, that too many public and private agencies have their hands in it, that each promotes its own interest and that the results are bad. On the contrary, however, its success is made possible in large measure by the very decentralization that prevails. Even so, various parts of agricultural research are over-organized. Directors of some of the largest state experiment stations cannot stay abreast of the changes in economic conditions within the state, of the complementary ongoing research in other parts of the University in which they are situated and, more important, of the implications and potentials of the research hypotheses advanced by agricultural scientists who are members of the experiment stations staff. In the major research universities in which a substantial part has agricultural relevance, the dean or whoever is in charge is also burdened by over-organization with consequences akin to those of large state experiment stations.

Thus, contrary to the Winrock report, U.S. agriculture would benefit from more, not less, decentralization. The report is distressed by the fact that, "At least ten federal agencies, in addition to the U.S. Department of Agriculture, now fund research pertinent to agriculture." Would that there were more for it would increase the competition in the research that gets done. The same logic applies for more funds from industry for agricultural research. The decentralization of agricultural research by states and within states, by universities and by regional specialized centres is a marked advantage. But farmers who provide the ultimate test of the value of research results in actual production are often correct in their assessment that the agricultural research on which they are dependent is not sufficiently decentralized to take adequate account of the farmer's ultimate test.

Advances in the sciences in physics, chemistry and biology are indeed important. The gains from specialization in research are well known. There are many organized research enterprises that specialized in each of the sciences. Agricultural research scientists are not slow in taking advantage of the advances in the sciences. They also from time to time contribute to these advances. But agricultural research is not research in the sciences *per se*.

Changes in agricultural research opportunities occur at a rapid pace. In some respects these opportunities are not being fully realized. Would that *Science for Agriculture* had been based on the competent study, *Agricultural Research Policy*, by Vernon W. Ruttan.[5] It would not have been flawed by the doctrine of centralized control for agricultural research. It would also have seen the many elements of strength along with several elements of weakness that characterize agricultural research.

IN CLOSING, A LITTLE LIST OF ISSUES

I shall state them briefly for discussions agenda.

1. When it comes to agricultural research in low income countries, agricultural scientists know more about the required research technology than most economists know about the economics of agricultural research applicable to these countries.

2. The research value of the feedback of information from farmers is underrated.

3. The benefits from agricultural research in a considerable number of low income countries are foreclosed by distortions in agricultural incentives. Most agricultural scientists still seem to be unaware of this fact.

4. The economic importance of free trade among countries is greatly underrated. Economists in the World Bank, under Anne Krueger's leadership, are now forthright on this issue. Reducing the barriers to trade would very much enhance the returns to agricultural research.

5. For any agency, here or abroad, to be granted an element of monopoly control of the market and of the distribution of new high yielding crop varieties results in a severe loss. On this issue, Canada errs as do many low income countries.

6. The marked decline in leadership in promoting and supporting new high quality agricultural research by the two major foundations is a decidedly adverse development. The Ford Foundation in its contribution to agriculture peaked during Frosty Hill's years. Social reforms now dominate. The Rockefeller Foundation with its long history of major contributions to agriculture, which peaked while George Harrar was President, is now also bent on fostering social reforms.

7. Canada's International Development Research Centre (IDRC), during the years when I knew it best, was first-rate and on a par with the high performance of the Rockefeller Foundation under Harrar. In its program for agriculture, food and nutrition, the leadership of Joseph Hulse deserves a high mark.

8. Given the fact that economic conditions are constantly changing and that the advances in the sciences are the order of the day, research entrepreneurship is exceedingly important. Is there a new generation of agricultural research entrepreneurs on a par with Richard Bradfield, Paul C. Mangelsdorf, E.C. Stakman, George J. Harrar, F.F. Hill, Norman E. Borlaug, Henry A. Wallace, Ralph Cumming, John Crawford, W. David Hopper, John D. Black and R.E. Buchanan of Iowa to whom I am greatly indebted? This is my no means an exhaustive list.[6] Is there such a new crop?

9. When it comes to farmers who have the acquired ability to deal efficiently with the increasingly complex technology of farming and with the changing economic conditions, the importance of their human capital — i.e., education, robust health and experience — is much underrated.

10. Another component of human capital consists of the specialized acquired skills of agricultural scientists and of economists who concentrate on agriculture. Although last on my little list it is by no means least in importance.

NOTES

1. From James K. Boyce and Robert E. Evenson, *National and International Agricultural Research and Extension Programs* (New York, Agricultural Development Council, 1975); and from M. Ann Judd, James K. Boyce, and Robert E. Evenson, "Investing in Agricultural Supply" (Economic Growth Center, Yale University, 1983), an unpublished paper.

2. Norman E. Borlaug, "The Green Revolution: Can we Make it Meet Expectations?" *Proceedings of the American Phytopathological Society* 3 (1976).

3. For an extended analysis of these centres, see Vernon W. Ruttan, *Agricultural Research Policy* (University of Minnesota Press, 1982), Chapter 5.

4. *Science for Agriculture*, report of a workshop held at Winrock, June 14-15, 1982, and published by the Rockefeller Foundation, New York, 1982. Here I draw on my review of it to appear in *Minerva*.

5. Vernon W. Ruttan, *Agricultural Research Policy* (Minneapolis: University of Minnesota Press, 1982), xiv + 369 pages.

6. See Henry A. Wallace, and William L. Brown, *Corn and Its Early Fathers* (Michigan State University Press, 1956); E.C. Stakman, Richard Bradfield, and Paul C. Mangelsdorf, *Campaigns Against Hunger* (Harvard University Press, 1967).

CHAPTER 3

THE CANADIAN AGRICULTURAL RESEARCH INSTITUTION

A. A. Guitard

INTRODUCTION

The research that led to expansion and diversification of agriculture in eastern and central Canada and that made possible the development of a stable agriculture in western Canada was started 100 years ago. The first seventy-five years were devoted primarily to building the research institution and to doing production research and taking the results to the producer. During the last twenty-five years there has been increasing emphasis on doing research for the whole food system, on scientific endeavour and on rationalizing, reorganizing and coordinating the research institution. This recent emphasis makes our discussions most timely and appropriate.

There are now 1,800 professionals doing research for Canadian agriculture. Some 900 are employed by the Government of Canada, 600 by provinces and universities and 300 are employed by industry. This is the basis for the assumption that 50 percent of the research done in Canada for agriculture is done by the Federal Government, 35 percent is done by provinces and universities and 15 percent by industry. This proportioning of research endeavour is influenced by a number of other factors and to this extent may not be valid. However, it does provide a useful impression of the division of research activities undertaken in support of agriculture in Canada. I would suggest that you keep these proportions in mind as I discuss the four components of the Canadian Agricultural Research Institution.

I wish to describe the research and development activities and attitudes of four major performers. I use numbers but no tables or charts because this is not a statistical evaluation. Numbers are used to give an indication of size and activity. I also discuss the origin of the numerous research units. I do this because only one unit is over 100 years old and the attitudes of many still reflect their heritage. And finally, I attempt to indicate how the individual research units or groups of units select and coordinate their research activities because I feel that this is one of the most useful indicators of attitude.

The information that I will present to you was obtained directly from the deputy ministers, deans and other senior administrators responsible for the research. Where appropriate I used their comments directly and elsewhere based my comments on their statements. The names of those who provided information are listed at the end of the presentation. I thank all for their assistance.

DEVELOPMENT

The first publicly-funded agricultural experiments were conducted at the School of Agriculture established in 1859 by Laval University at Ste. Anne de la Pocatière in Quebec. This was followed by comparisons of cultivars of crops and breeds of animals at the Ontario Agricultural College soon after it was established by the Ontario Department of Agriculture at Guelph in 1874. The Government of Canada commenced to exercise a national responsibility for agricultural research with the appointment of a dominion entomologist in 1884. Canada became actively involved in research for agriculture with the creation of the Experimental Farm Service in 1886. This was the beginning of the Canadian Agricultural Research Institution.

Despite its pioneering status, Canada was not far behind Europe and the United States in recognizing the need for and value of agricultural research. In England, Rothamstead, regarded by many as the "Mother of Experimental Stations," commenced experiments in 1843. Organized experiments with crops and animals were started in Germany in 1852 and in France in 1878. In the United States, Michigan established an agricultural college with research facilities in 1857. Land grant colleges, some with experimental stations, were established in 1862 by the Morrill Act. In 1882, only four years before the establishment of the Experimental Farm Service in Canada, the Hatch Act in the United States provided for land grants to a system of state experiment stations.

In Canada, there was very active expansion of research capability during the early 1900s. This was a direct response to need. Faculties and colleges of agriculture were opened to train professionals. Research was commenced as a natural adjunct to teaching. The Experimental Farm Service started a number of experimental farms and stations. The Department of Agriculture created a new Science Service to do more basic research than was usually desirable on experimental farms. As the century progressed the National Research Council was formed and developed research programs in areas relating to agriculture. The Prairie Farm Rehabilitation Administration was developed in response to the prairie drought and commenced to fund dryland research. The provinces developed agricultural extension services and occasionally initiated applied research in support of selected activities. Industry became involved in agricultural research in Canada both directly and by providing resources for existing programs.

There was a surge of growth following World War II. This was followed by a maturing of the research institution that is still continuing. It is marked by consolidations, specialization, modification, rationalization and preoccupation with coordination. It is also marked by conflict and identity crises. Canada created a Ministry of State for Science and Technology; strengthened the Agricultural Services Coordinating Committee by developing a Canadian Agricultural Research Council and expert committees; amalgamated the experimental farm and science services to form the Research Branch with responsibility for all agricultural research except economics and veterinary medicine, and developed a Regional Development and International Affairs Branch with responsibility for research relating to regional and international development. Faculties and colleges of agriculture diversified and intensified their research activities and in various ways established research programs that are essentially separate from their teaching functions. Provinces became more actively involved in agricultural research both directly and by funding programs being conducted by others. Industry became more involved with research and is now doing research independently, under contract and by funding research institutions. Plant breeders rights are still being debated. Farm organizations are attempting to form a Western Grains Research Foundation. And so the reaching for maturity continues.

THE FEDERAL COMPONENT

The Government of Canada is responsible for 50 percent of the agricultural research in Canada. The majority of the research is done by Agriculture Canada under authority of the Department of Agriculture Act of 1886, the Experimental Farms Stations Act of 1886, an Act Respecting Contagious Diseases of Animals passed in 1879 and the Canada Grains Act of 1930. Under these authorities the research is undertaken by the Research Branch, the Animal Pathology Division of the Health of Animals Directorate of the Food Production and Inspection Branch, and the Grain Research Laboratory of the Canadian Grain Commission. Other departments and agencies of the Government of Canada occasionally fund, undertake or cooperate in research that has application to agriculture, but their small and infrequent activities will not be discussed. The only other agency that has a significant involvement with agricultural research is the National Research Council of Canada.

RESEARCH BRANCH

The Research Branch was started in 1886 as the Experimental Farm Service with a mandate to solve problems relating to agricultural production and make the results known to producers. The Act authorized the establishment of experimental farms at Ottawa, Ontario; Nappan, Nova Scotia; Brandon, Manitoba; Indian Head, Saskatchewan; and Agassiz, British Columbia. All of the farms were operational by 1890, but agriculture was expanding and it was soon realized that these five were not enough. From the early 1900s until approximately 1945 a number of new farms and stations were established. During this period a Science Service was developed by the Department of Agriculture to do more basic research than was usually appropriate on experimental farms. The Science Service developed laboratories throughout Canada. The two services were amalgamated in 1959 to form the Research Branch of Agriculture Canada.

Since 1959 the Branch has undergone many changes in program, administrative procedure and operational philosophy. Operationally, the most significant change was a decision in 1978 to divide the Branch into semi-autonomous regions. There are now five regions, each administered by a director general. These directors general and the Director General for Program Planning and Evaluation form a Branch Management Committee that advises the Assistant Deputy Minister (Research) on all matters relating to the research needs and operational requirements of the Branch.

In this manner the Branch conducts research in all areas of agricultural endeavour except infectious diseases of animals and product and market related economics. In 1982-83 the research was conducted at sixty-one locations extending across Canada. There were five institutes, twenty-six research stations, two research centres, twelve experimental farms and sixteen sub-stations. The institutes, research stations and research centres are the main research units that report directly to a regional director general. The regions and main research units were distributed in the following manner during 1982-83: the Institute region with headquarters in Ottawa had the Chemistry and Biology Research Institute, Land Resource Research Institute, Engineering and Statistical Research Institute, Food Research Institute, Biosystematics Research Institute and the Research Program Services all located in Ottawa; the Atlantic region with headquarters in Halifax had research stations at St. John's in Newfoundland, Charlottetown in Prince Edward Island, Kentville in Nova Scotia and Fredericton in New Brunswick; the Quebec region with headquarters in Montreal had research stations at St.-Jean, Ste.-Foy and Lennoxville; the Ontario region with headquarters in Ottawa had research stations in Ottawa, London, Vineland, Delhi and Harrow and the Animal Research Centre in Ottawa; and the Western region with headquarters in Saskatoon had research stations at Brandon, Morden and Winnipeg in Manitoba, Melfort, Regina, Saskatoon and Swift Current in Saskatchewan, Beaverlodge, Lacombe and Lethbridge in Alberta and Agassiz, Kamloops, Saanichton, Summerland and Vancouver in British Columbia.

In 1982-83 the Branch was staffed by 917 professionals and 2,730 person-years of support staff for a total of 3,647 person-years. The professionals were distributed among branch objectives as follows: land - 87, water - 22, energy - 6, environmental quality - 20, animal production - 102, crop production - 369, production support - 197, farm input supply - 7, processing - 34, distribution - 10, food quality and nutrition - 13 and administrative support - 50.

The research branch budget for the 1982-83 fiscal year was $177 million. Of this, $119 million was used to pay salaries and wages, $28 million was used for operation and maintenance of the research units, $19 million was used to purchase new buildings and equipment, $9 million was used to purchase contract research from universities and industry and $2 million was granted to universities in aid of research. It is estimated that the Research Branch received approximately $2 million worth of assistance from the provinces and a further $2 million from industry in the form of goods and services. The largest contributor was the Province of Alberta through their Farming for the Future program.

Selection and coordination of research initiatives is accomplished in a number of ways. At the national level, major areas of activity are initiated by Agriculture Canada on the advice of many people including the Senior Management Committee of the Department. The Assistant Deputy Minister (Research) is a member of this Committee. Within the Research Branch, programs are modified and new programs are structured on the recommendation of the Director General Program Planning and Evaluation and his ten coordinators and with the advice of the regional directors general. Regional programs are initiated and modified in a similar manner within the established program authorities of the regional directors general. Projects required to meet program responsibilities are initiated and modified as required by station, institute and centre directors with the advice of scientists and regional and national program personnel. The whole process is based on a sequence of annual commitments for research and a process whereby each individual scientist is responsible to the Deputy Minister for a designated part of the mandate of the Research Branch and is accountable annually through his Director, Director General and Assistant Deputy Minister.

Considerable international coordination is accomplished by the Assistant Deputy Minister (Research) and his directors general meeting with their counterparts in the United States, England and France every two years to discuss problems in agriculture and the research required for their solution. This is supplemented by a number of individual contacts throughout the world and by scientists working for one-year periods at major research establishments in a number of countries.

The Canadian Agricultural Services Coordinating Committee and its Canadian Agricultural Research Council, provincial agricultural services coordinating committees and expert committees form the basis for the coordination of research done by the Research Branch, provinces and universities. This is supplemented by workshops and group and individual consultation and communication at the national, regional and station level.

ANIMAL PATHOLOGY DIVISION

The Division has its roots in the foresight of a Montreal veterinarian who, in 1875, persuaded the Government of Canada that quarantine and legislation to prevent the introduction of diseases from Europe was needed to protect Canadian cattle. In the beginning the required research was done at Canadian universities by a few part-time veterinarians funded by the Department of Agriculture. By 1902 a branch of the Department had been created and a laboratory provided on the Central Experimental Farm in Ottawa.

There is now a headquarters in Ottawa and eight laboratories which include the Animal Disease Research Institute in Nepean (Ottawa), Ontario and Lethbridge, Alberta, and animal pathology laboratories in Vancouver, British Columbia; Saskatoon, Saskatchewan; Winnipeg, Manitoba; Guelph, Ontario; Saint-Hyacinthe, Quebec; and Sackville, New Brunswick. Five are involved in research as well as providing diagnostic services.

The research conducted in the animal pathology laboratories or funded by the Animal Pathology Division is in support of the National Animal Health program which is concerned with detecting and preventing animal disease entry into Canada, controlling and irradicating animal diseases in Canada, and surveying Canadian animals for disease. The research priorities arising from these objectives relate to foreign animal diseases, identified indigenous diseases, non-program indigenous diseases and meat safety.

During the 1982-83 fiscal year the Division had a staff of 120 of which forty-one were professionals, mostly veterinarians. The budget for the year was $4.7 million spent in support of research at the five locations that do research.

The proposals for research put forward by divisional personnel are approved by the Associate Director of Research. The priorities of the Division and the needs of the agricultural industry determine the selection. Industry needs are identified mainly through the Canadian Agricultural Services Coordinating Committee. It has several sub-committees that function, in part, as a monitor of industry needs.

GRAIN RESEARCH LABORATORY

The Laboratory is operated by the Canadian Grain Commission that was established by the Canada Grain Act of 1912 and has its roots in the Manitoba Grain Act of 1900. It was established to regulate the warehousing, transport and marketing of prairie cereals and to undertake other responsibilities that would stabilize the industry. It was required to impose tariffs to support its operation.

In 1913 the Commission established the Grain Research Laboratory which is financed by Agriculture Canada. The mandate of the Laboratory is to assess the quality of each year's crop, monitor the quality of shipments of cereals and oilseeds, assist plant breeders in evaluating quality of breeding material, conduct research in the processing of cereals and oilseeds, provide technical services to the Commission and the Canadian Wheat Board and assist sales agencies in technical matters relating to the quality of cereals and oilseeds. Research relating to these responsibilities is conducted with cereal grains including hard red spring wheat, durum wheat, soft white spring wheat, soft white winter wheat, red winter wheat and barley, and with oilseeds including flax, rape seed (canola), sunflowers and soybeans.

During the 1982-83 fiscal year the Laboratory had a staff of ninety. The professional staff consisted of the Director, ten scientists, five chemists, a statistician and an information officer. The operating budget was $3.5 million.

Research priorities are dictated by identified problems that are within the mandate of the Laboratory. They are mostly established by individuals in discussion with the Director and the Chief Commissioner of the Canadian Grain Commission. The Director and some scientists are members of a number of the expert committees that report to the Canadian Agricultural Services Coordinating Committee. This provides external information and coordination.

NATIONAL RESEARCH COUNCIL

The National Research Council (NRC) was established in 1916 by an act of Parliament. Agriculture was included in its mandate. In the early years of development it was primarily advisory and undertook certain coordinating functions. In this capacity it established in the early 1940s the associate committees that each year brought together federal and university scientists working in all disciplines required for the development of cereal and oilseed varieties. This activity was later transferred to the Canadian Agricultural Services Coordinating Committee. The associate committees and their sub-committees became the Crop Production and Expert committees.

During the 1930s the Council commenced to develop its own laboratories. These were established in Ottawa, Halifax and Saskatoon. The laboratory in Saskatoon was first housed in a university building. In 1948 the NRC constructed its own building on the campus of the University of Saskatchewan and established the Prairie Regional Laboratory. It was often involved in research relating to agriculture, including the research that assisted in establishing rapeseed as a crop. In May 1983 the Prairie Regional Laboratory became the Plant Biotechnology Institute with plans for expansion that will enhance its capability to do basic research relating to agriculture.

During 1982-83 the Laboratory did research relating to the biology and biochemistry, criobiology and cloning and molecular genetics of plant cells, plant energetics, microphyte metabolism, organic chemistry, chemical ecology and plant utilization. In total, sixty-eight members of the staff were involved in this research, of which thirty-two were scientists. The laboratory budget for 1982-83 was $7.1 million.

The Plant Biotechnology Institute is a division of the National Research Council. It is operated by a divisional director who has the authority to modify programs within existing mandates and resources. New programs are developed and costed on a five-year basis and forwarded for consideration by a selection committee consisting of randomly selected divisional directors and scientists and chaired by a vice-president of the Council. The initial need for the modification of existing programs or development of new programs is based on knowledge of the industries served. This knowledge is obtained in many ways including membership in the Canadian Agricultural Services Coordinating Committee.

THE PROVINCIAL COMPONENT

The Canadian provinces support agricultural research in various ways. Alberta, Ontario and Quebec have their own research programs. These three provinces and British Columbia, Saskatchewan, Manitoba and Nova Scotia support agricultural research at their universities. All provinces do adaptation and demonstration research as part of their extension programs. All cooperate with the Research Branch of Agriculture Canada and with producers and processors in the province. A few, particularly Alberta, assist the Research Branch.

All provincial deputy ministers of agriculture are active members of the Canadian Agricultural Services Coordinating Committee (CASCC) and chair a provincial agricultural services coordinating committee. Each provincial committee has a member on the Canadian Agricultural Research Council (CARC). This provides coordination of activities.

It is generally agreed that provinces and universities now do some 35 percent of the agricultural research in Canada. Arrangements for financing and staffing of universities by provinces vary widely. Provinces fund other agencies and universities do not receive all of their funding from provinces. This makes it virtually impossible to apportion the 35 percent between universities and provinces.

Regardless, it is desirable to consider provinces and universities as separate components of the Canadian Agricultural Research Institution because they have very different attitudes toward research. The university attitude is essentially academic and the provincial attitude is essentially practical, applied and user-oriented.

BRITISH COLUMBIA

The British Columbia Ministry of Agriculture and Food has been involved in diverse programs of agricultural research for the past thirty years. Many of the projects are demonstrational.

The 1982-83 expenditure was $491,400 on 263 projects. In descending order of number of projects, the research was concerned with field crops, horticulture, crop protection, soils, engineering, poultry, apiary, economics, livestock, veterinary and information. Fourteen projects were conducted under a federal Agricultural Research and Development Agreement (ARDA) and eighteen were Regional Extension Service projects. A number of projects were under the Demonstration of Agricultural Technology and Economics (DATE) program which was initiated in 1974 to "make available funds to assist in the introduction of advanced agricultural and economic technique to the food supply system."

The projects are mostly cooperative with Agriculture Canada, the University of British Columbia, industry, producer organizations and individual producers. Ministry staff are involved in most of the projects. Initiation and coordination are usually by agreement among several individuals. Identification of areas of concern is often the result of recognition of areas of deficiency through discussions at meetings of the British Columbia Agricultural Services Coordinating Committee (BCASCC) and its lead committees.

ALBERTA

Alberta Agriculture has been involved in agricultural research and development since 1935 when it assumed responsibility for what is now the Horticultural Research Centre at Brooks. It now operates this Centre and a Field Crops Research Facility at Lacombe. The province employs some fifty-five scientists at these two locations. A wide variety of crop research is conducted at these centres. Alberta Agriculture also operates service laboratories in Lethbridge, Airdrie, Fairview and Edmonton. Alberta Agriculture is closely associated with the Alberta Environment Centre at Vegreville that does research for Agriculture. A new Food Processing Development Centre is presently under construction at Leduc, financed by a $7.7 million allocation from the Heritage Savings Trust Fund.

The 1982-83 expenditure on research was estimated at $17.8 million. In excess of $5.7 million of this was spent in support of research under the Farming for the Future program. Except for the research at Brooks and Lacombe this program is Alberta Agriculture's major research initiative.

Farming for the Future is an Alberta Heritage Fund program that was created in October 1977. It has provided in excess of $25 million for agricultural research for Alberta. In 1982-83 there were 150 projects covering all agricultural commodities and conducted in provincial, university, federal and industry research facilities. The accumulated expenditure on these projects since 1979 is $15 million. Under an Agreement for Cooperation between Agriculture Canada and Alberta Agriculture, some $4.1 million of this expenditure provided assistance to the Research Branch in conducting thirty-six projects.

The benefits of the research must accrue to agriculture in Alberta but some research is funded outside of the province. The program is being continued and expanded. Expansion will include on-farm research demonstration and adaptation and a graduate student research support program intended to provide graduate students with up to $10 thousand to cover thesis research costs.

Farming for the Future and its sub-programs are managed by the Agricultural Research Council of Alberta (ARCA) created in 1978. The Minister of Agriculture is chairman and the Council has fifteen members consisting of eight producers and seven representatives from Alberta Agriculture, Agriculture Canada, the University of Alberta, the Research Council of Alberta and the Legislative Assembly of Alberta.

The Alberta Agricultural Services Coordinating Committee (AASCC) and advisory committees are charged with the broader responsibility of integration of federal, provincial, university and industry research and service programs.

SASKATCHEWAN

The Saskatchewan Department of Agriculture has a long history of support of applied developmental research by their own staff and by grants to others. Recently they have developed three specific programs to meet the research needs of Saskatchewan's agricultural industry. These are the Market Development Fund developed in 1974, the Saskatchewan Agricultural Research Fund commenced in 1980 and FarmLab initiated in 1981. Funding of all research activities totalled $4.8 million during the 1982-83 fiscal year.

Approximately $50 thousand was used by departmental staff working alone and in cooperation with Agriculture Canada and producers in support of research in livestock, irrigation and mechanization. Approximately $400 thousand was awarded in contracts and grants for research with blackflies, irrigation and production and processing economics. Approximately $1.2 million was granted to the Agricultural Machinery Institute of which $50 thousand was used for research. The Market Development Fund awarded $55 thousand for product development studies. The Saskatchewan Agricultural Research Fund paid out $590 thousand during 1982-83 in support of thirty-seven projects, mostly in crops and livestock. FarmLab spent $115 thousand on producer initiated projects and awarded contracts totalling $3.5 million to the University of Saskatchewan. Some of the university funds were transferred to the Institute of Pedology, Crop Development Centre, Prairie Swine Research Centre, POS Pilot Plant (Protein, Oil, Starch) and VIDO (Veterinary Infectious Diseases Organization).

The Research Fund was established in response to a perceived need for increased support of agricultural research by the Province and to allow for direct producer input into the decision-making process. The interest from a $3.2 million capital fund is awarded annually by the board on the basis of potential benefit to agriculture in Saskatchewan. This board is comprised of four producers, two agricultural researchers and a departmental representative.

FarmLab was initiated to combine the expertise of researchers and producers in research and demonstration in an attempt to transfer agricultural research results to producers more rapidly. Producers may initiate projects or cooperate on university initiated projects. Producer plans are approved by regional committees after being approved by agricultural committees at the municipal level and by the local agricultural representative. University proposals are approved at meetings of the Associate Dean of Agriculture and department heads.

Broad coordination of the research is a function of the Saskatchewan Agricultural Services Coordinating Committee (SASCC) and its advisory committees.

MANITOBA

Manitoba Agriculture has maintained a long-standing interest in and involvement with applied agricultural research. The involvement is mostly through support of the Faculty of Agriculture of the University of Manitoba. An ongoing year-by-year grant is provided to the Faculty without specifying the research projects or activities to be conducted. Formal and informal consultations between the Department and the Faculty do take place at which time research and investigation priorities are discussed, planned and reported. The Faculty most often uses the funds to respond more quickly to identified needs and to conduct a larger and more "Manitoba oriented" research program than would otherwise be possible. The Manitoba Agriculture grant to the University was about $850 thousand during the 1982-83 fiscal year. It has risen to that level in small increments from a grant of approximately $500 thousand in 1963.

When appropriate, the Department also funds specific and well-defined research activities, again primarily at the University of Manitoba. In the last four years the Federal-Provincial Subsidiary Agreement on Value-Added Crop Production (Agro-Man) has provided funding ranging from $400 thousand to $700 thousand per year for projects that test basic research results in the commercial environment in order to develop recommendations that can be used by producers. Sixty percent of the funds are co-shared with the Government of Canada.

The Department, through other budget areas, also contracts for smaller, more specific research projects or studies primarily with the University of Manitoba. Annual expenditure for these contracts normally ranges from $50 thousand to $100 thousand per year. There are other projects, some under Agro-Man, which involve producer groups that are investigational but are not classed as research. These are concerned with adaptation of technology and illustration of new and improved crop and livestock management techniques. These extension-oriented activities are an attempt to rapidly bring known research results to farm application.

The general direction to research and related activities is given by the Manitoba Agricultural Services Coordinating Committee (MASCC) and its associated subcommittees.

ONTARIO

The Ontario Ministry of Agriculture and Food (OMAF) has been involved in agricultural research since 1874 when, as the Ontario Department of Agriculture, it established the Ontario Agricultural College and Experimental Farm at Guelph. It subsequently established the Ontario Veterinary College and the Macdonald Institute. The Department managed these three institutions until 1965 when they became colleges of the newly-formed University of Guelph. The research and service components of the programs of the three colleges continue to receive major funding from OMAF. OMAF also funds the Horticultural Research Institute of Ontario which has experimental stations at Bradford, Simcoe and Vineland, and research at colleges of Agricultural Technology at Kemptville, New Liskeard and Ridgetown that do research. In total, OMAF funds research, in whole or in part, at twelve establishments in Ontario. The 1982-83 OMAF expenditure at these locations exceeded $29 million in support of research conducted by 153 professionals. The 1983 research priorities cover a number of aspects of integrated soil and crop management practices; integrated pest control systems for horticultural and field crops; integrated animal production systems; high quality Ontario foods; agricultural economics; and biotechnology as it applies to crop and livestock production and food processing.

OMAF commenced formal coordination of its research with the appointment of a Director of Research in 1948. In 1962 the Agricultural Institute of Ontario (ARIO) was created to inquire into programs of research with respect to agriculture, veterinary medicine and household science; to select and recommend areas of research for the betterment of agriculture, veterinary medicine and household science; and to stimulate interest in research as a means of developing in Ontario a high degree of efficiency in the production and marketing of agricultural products. The ARIO is composed largely of members representing agricultural producers and agribusiness and is charged with direct responsibility for the expenditure of OMAF funds for research. It is a decision-making body concerned with giving direction to research programs directly under the control of OMAF.

The Ontario Agricultural Services Coordinating Committee (OASCC) and its eight committees are charged with the broader responsibility of integration of federal, provincial, university and industry research and service programs in Ontario. It was formed in 1966 and has as members the heads of all Ontario-based agricultural research institutions.

QUEBEC

The Ministère de l'Agriculture des Pêcheries et l'Alimentation (Department of Agriculture, Fisheries and Food) has been involved in agricultural research since a bureau de l'entomologie was founded in 1913. This grew into a large, well-coordinated La direction de la recherche (Research Branch) that in 1973 was incorporated into a Direction Générale (Research and Education). It now consists of three services and four research stations that in 1982-83 employed sixty-eight professionals and had an operating budget of $9.9 million.

The three services have been located in the Complexe scientifique in Quebec City since 1971. The Plant Protection Service is concerned with all activities with a plant protection implication and coordination of these activities, the Soil Service with soil classification, mapping and soil fertility, and the Food Technology Service works in close cooperation with industry. There are four research stations. The most northerly station, Les Buissons, works exclusively with potatoes; Déchambault works with animals; Saint-Hyacinthe is mostly concerned with cereals, and horticultural crops, and La Pocatière works with early cultivars of corn and soybeans and has large programs with fababeans and broad beans.

Coordination of research activities is based on a well-defined accountability: Deputy Minister - Assistant Deputy Minister (Research and Administration) - Research Director - Directors of Research Services and Stations. The process for setting of research priorities is equally well defined but more complex. It involves Le Conseil des Recherches et des Services Agricole du Québec (CRSAQ) (The Quebec Agricultural Research and Services Council). Setting of priorities also involves the Plant, Animal and Food Production Councils and their numerous committees which provide the forum for scientists, industry and extension representatives to discuss research needs.

Le Conseil des Recherches et des Services Agricole du Québec (CRSAQ) started in 1936 as the Comité des Recherches Agricole (Agricultural Research Committee) and in 1947 the Conseil des Recherches Agricole (Agricultural Research Council). Commencing in 1943 it was concerned with scholarships for post-graduate training and after 1963 it became more structured and commenced to play a role in supporting research in agricultural colleges. It attained its present form in 1973 as a very major council chaired by the Deputy Minister and with members consisting of the Quebec Director of Research, directors of the three federal research stations, representatives from the three production councils as well as representatives from Quebec Agricultural Services, Fisheries and Education. As well as the usual coordinating and federal liaison activities it is required to advise the Department on the allocation of research grants to professors of the faculties of Agriculture and Veterinary Medicine. During 1982-83 grants totalled $2.5 million and fifteen M.Sc. assistantships were awarded.

The Quebec Agricultural Research and Services Council, through its composition, acts as a medium of coordination on a voluntary basis of research efforts by the three main components: provincial, federal and university representatives.

NEW BRUNSWICK

The New Brunswick Department of Agriculture and Rural Development is involved in a number of activities designed to adapt the results of research to on-farm applications and to transfer new technology to farmers. New Brunswick depends almost exclusively on Agriculture Canada for its agricultural research, except in areas relating particularly to New Brunswick. Examples are research with fiddle-heads, apple canker and soil erosion. These are an integral part of the Department's demonstration and extension activities and are not budgeted separately.

New Brunswick is a member of the Atlantic Agricultural Services Coordinating Committee (AASCC) and thus is involved in setting research priorities for the whole Atlantic region.

NOVA SCOTIA

The Nova Scotia Department of Agriculture and Marketing (NSDA&M) supports research at the Nova Scotia Agricultural College and its extension service con-ducts demonstration and adaptation projects in support of extension. In 1982-83 the Department funded thirty-three projects at the Nova Scotia Agricultural Col-lege (NSAC) with an expenditure of $168 thousand. Projects were with horticul-tural crops, cereals, forages, livestock, poultry, engineering, etc.

The Department has had a research committee since 1969. The principal function of the committee is to review applications for research funds. It is composed of nine people. The Chairman and three others are senior NSAC faculty, four are senior NSDA&M staff and the other is the Assistant Director of the Agriculture Canada Research Station at Kentville.

Nova Scotia is a member of the Atlantic Agricultural Services Coordinating Committee (AASCC) and thus is involved in setting research priorities for the whole Atlantic region.

PRINCE EDWARD ISLAND

The Department of Agriculture and Forestry has a number of demonstration plots but does not consider these to be research. All of the research is conducted by the Canada Agriculture Research Station at Charlottetown. Under a Federal-Provincial Comprehensive Development Plan that extended from 1969 to 1983 the Depart-ment assisted with setting priorities for expenditure of funds made available by the Department of Regional Economic Expansion (DREE).

Prince Edward Island is a member of the Atlantic Agricultural Services Coordi-nating Committee (AASCC)and thus is involved in setting research priorities for the whole Atlantic region.

NEWFOUNDLAND AND LABRADOR

The Department of Rural, Agricultural and Northern Development does not give financial support to research but does cooperate in numerous research-related scientific activities and the transfer of the technology to the small farming community. The Department identifies industry requirements for research, brings these to the attention of the Canada Agriculture Research Station and, when appropriate, cooperates in the solution of the problems.

Newfoundland is a member of the Atlantic Agricultural Services Coordinating Committee (AASCC) and thus is involved in setting research priorities for the whole Atlantic region.

THE UNIVERSITY COMPONENT

Eight Canadian universities and one agricultural college conduct agricultural research. The research is done in faculties of Agriculture and Veterinary Medicine. Other faculties of these universities and other universities may do research that has application to agriculture. However, it is not conceptually agricultural and is not considered in this presentation.

Most faculties were created early in the development of their university and were established with very strong support from the province in which they are located. Early in their development they undertook studies of local production problems with crops and animals. They were often the research arm of the province. Some continue in this capacity as well as undertaking the research associated with post-graduate training. Teaching and research are now mutually supportive activities in all faculties.

It is in this situation that universities, together with the provinces in which they are located, conduct 35 percent of the agricultural research in Canada.

UNIVERSITY OF BRITISH COLUMBIA

The agricultural research is conducted by the Faculty of Agricultural Sciences. It was established in 1915 as one of the three original faculties. Research was commenced early in the development of the Faculty particularly with cereals, grass seeds, vegetables and the development of a herd of Ayrshire cattle.

The Faculty now has departments of Agricultural Economics, Agricultural Mechanics and Bio-Engineering, Animal Science, Food Science, Plant Science, Poultry Science and Soil Science. All departments have broad research programs that tend to reflect the diversity of the agriculture in the province. The majority of the research is done on the campus. The Faculty also maintains a herd of Holstein cattle and does research on some 700 hectares of land located at Oyster River on Vancouver Island.

The Faculty has fifty-nine full-time professionals who do from fifteen to eighteen person-years of research. During the 1982-83 fiscal year there were 330 undergraduate and 120 graduate students. The operating budget for 1982-83 was $3.9 million. The operating budget was supplemented by $3.4 million received as funding for research. Agriculture Canada provided 26 percent of the funding for research, other federal agencies 50 percent, the province 19 percent, the university 2 percent and industry 3 percent. The Agriculture Canada funding was divided into 7 percent for research grants and 19 percent for research contracts.

The research is often conducted in cooperation with federal and provincial agencies and with industry. Within this framework of cooperation, research priorities are set by the departments. During development, projects are approved by the originating department, signed by the head and reviewed and signed by the dean. External coordination and direction is provided by the dean being a member of the British Columbia Agricultural Services Coordinating Committee (BCASCC) and senior staff members being members of the lead committees of BCASCC.

UNIVERSITY OF ALBERTA

The agricultural research is conducted by the Faculty of Agriculture and Forestry. The Faculty started in 1915 and soon commenced a research program. The Grey Wooded soil tests started at Breton in 1930 continue to be used. The research momentum has been building and there has been particularly large growth during the past ten years.

The Faculty now has departments of Agricultural Engineering, Animal Science, Entomology, Food Science, Forest Science, Plant Science (includes Horticulture), Rural Economy (includes Agricultural Economics and Rural Sociology) and Soil Science. The departments of Animal Science and Plant Science have the largest and most diversified research program but all departments have active programs. As well as doing research on the 280 hectare Edmonton Research Station, the Department of Animal Science operates a 3,000 hectare ranch at Kinsella, 150 kilometres southeast of Edmonton, and the Departments of Animal Science, Plant Science, Agricultural Engineering and Soil Science operate a 130 hectare research site at Ellerslie, twenty kilometres east of Edmonton. The Department of Animal Science also operates the sixty-six hectare Ministik Wildlife site, and Entomology has a sixty-six hectare lowland site at George Lake.

The Faculty had ninety-six academic staff and 550 undergraduate students during 1982-83. It is estimated that thirty person-years of professional staff time was devoted to research. Additionally, it is estimated that some 25 percent of the time of the 200 non-academic and 150 graduate students was devoted to conducting and supporting research. The net operating budget of the Faculty was $9.4 million during 1982-83. It is estimated that one-third or $3.1 million of this was used in support of research. This was supplemented by approximately $3.5 million of external funding (excluding Forestry). The Alberta Agriculture's Farming for the Future program provided 50 percent of the external funding in support of fifty-seven projects. The Alberta Agricultural Research Trust, with matching funds from industry, provided 10 percent. Agriculture Canada provided 3 percent of the research funding and other federal agencies 23 percent.

There is close cooperation with Alberta Agriculture, the Alberta Research Council, Agriculture Canada, industry and other faculties of the university. There are joint appointments with other faculties and there are staff members whose salaries are fully, or in part, paid by Alberta Agriculture and NSERC. Internal coordination of research is provided by all research grant applications requiring approval of the chairman of the department, the dean of the faculty and the Office of the Vice-President (Research). External coordination and direction is provided by the dean of the faculty being a member of the Alberta Agricultural

Services Coordinating Committee (AASCC) and senior professional staff being members of the advisory committees of AASCC.

UNIVERSITY OF SASKATCHEWAN

Agricultural research is conducted by the College of Agriculture and the Western College of Veterinary Medicine.

College of Agriculture

The College was started in 1911. As early as the 1920s the Government of Saskatchewan considered the College to be its agricultural research arm. During the early years it did the usual adaptation and demonstration research with particular attention to crop and animal production under conditions of insufficient moisture.

The College now has departments of Agricultural Economics, Animal and Poultry Science, Crop Science and Plant Ecology, Horticultural Science, Soil Science and Applied Microbiology and Food Science. All have strong research programs. Part of the research is undertaken by the Crop Development Centre, Institute of Pedology and Prairie Swine Centre that are directly associated with the College. In addition to the normal campus facilities, which include 180 hectares of plot land, the College owns and operates the University Farm (350 hectares), Goodale Farm (410 hectares shared with the Western College of Veterinary Medicine), Kernen Crop Research Farm (500 hectares) and the Biddulph Farm (125 hectares). The College also rents native rangeland at the Matador Research Station (755 hectares).

The College has a total staff of 280. Of these, sixty-one are professional teaching staff and forty-six are research associates mostly associated with the institute and centres. In 1982-83 there were 560 undergraduate degree students and 120 graduate students. The current operating budget of the College is approximately $6 million. An additional $6 million is received in external grants and contracts for research. Approximately 62 percent of the external funding for research is received from the Government of Saskatchewan mostly through the FarmLab program. Federal granting councils and departments, including Agriculture Canada, provide 30 percent and industry and others provide 8 percent.

Within a broad program framework, research projects are chosen by individual researchers in consultation with the sponsoring agency. The individual presents the project to a departmental committee for approval. The Saskatchewan Agricultural Services Coordinating Committee (SASCC), of which the dean is a member, and the network of SASCC committees, to which senior staff members belong, assure additional advice with regard to research needs and priorities.

Western College of Veterinary Medicine (WCVM)

The WCVM was established in 1965 as a regional institution to serve the four western provinces and the northern territories. A well-developed program of research was included in the original plans.

The College has departments of Anatomy, Physiological Sciences, Microbiology, Pathology, Anaesthesiology, Radiology and Surgery, Herd Medicine, and Theriogenology and Internal Medicine. The Veterinary Teaching Hospital co-ordinates the College's service activities. Research with beef cattle is emphasized but there is also research with sheep, swine, horses, companion animals and wildlife. In the research with food animals there is strong association with the Department of Animal and Poultry Science of the College of Agriculture.

During 1982-83 the College had a professional staff of seventy-three, 265 undergraduate and seventy-six graduate students. In 1981-82 the College received $1.6 million in external funding for research. Federal agencies provided 41 percent of this, provincial agencies 40 percent, industry 1 percent and foundations and individuals 18 percent. The provincial support was provided by Alberta 24 percent, Saskatchewan 12 percent and Ontario 4 percent.

The College works with the four western provinces in establishing research priorities. The association is primarily through the provincial agricultural services coordinating committees and their subcommittees.

UNIVERSITY OF MANITOBA

The agricultural research is conducted by the Faculty of Agriculture. The Faculty was commenced in 1906 but research did not become a major endeavour until the mid-1950s.

The Faculty has departments of Agricultural Economics and Farm Management, Agricultural Engineering, Animal Science, Entomology, Food Science, Plant Science and Soil Science. All departments have active research programs. The Faculty operates the Glenlea Research Station, a 525 hectare facility located twenty-one kilometres south of the University.

During 1982-83 the Faculty had some ninety academic and teaching staff and a further eighty full and part-time professionals attached to the Faculty. There were 580 undergraduate degree students, 268 graduate students and 145 non-academic support staff. The operating budget of the Faculty was $7 million during 1982-83. In 1982-83 this was supplemented by $4 million of external funding for research. Manitoba Agriculture provided 22 percent of the research funding directly and 17 percent on a shared basis with the federal Department of Regional Economic Expansion through Agro-Man contracts. Other departments of the Government of Manitoba provided 5 percent. NSERC provided 24 percent, Agriculture Canada 9 percent and other agencies of the Government of Canada 10 percent. Industry and other support provided 13 percent of the funding.

There is extensive and continuous cooperation with the Manitoba Department of Agriculture. For many years there has been close association and cooperation with the Agriculture Canada research station on campus and many of its senior staff are adjunct professors. More recently, similar arrangements were made with the Freshwater Institute of Environment Canada which is also located on the campus. Plant scientists have associated closely with the Grain Research Laboratory of the Canadian Grain Commission in Winnipeg and with the Provincial Food Products Laboratory at Portage la Prairie.

Most research decisions are made by individual departments. However, since the Faculty has been designated the research arm of the Manitoba Department of Agriculture and receives major funding from this source, continuous consultation is maintained. Also, the Manitoba Agricultural Services Coordinating Committee (MASCC), of which the dean is a member, and the network of MASCC committees, to which senior staff members belong, assure additional advice and consultations with regard to research needs and priorities.

UNIVERSITY OF GUELPH

Agricultural research is conducted by the Ontario Agricultural College and the Ontario Veterinary College both of which are part of the University.

Ontario Agricultural College (OAC)

The College was founded in 1874 by the Ontario Department of Agriculture and was operated by the Department until 1964 when it became a college of the newly-formed University of Guelph. Agricultural research commenced with the founding of the College and has expanded continuously.

The College now has departments of Animal and Poultry Science, Environmental Biology, Horticultural Science, Crop Science, Food Science and Land Resource Science. It also has schools of Agricultural Economics and Extension Education, Engineering and Landscape Architecture. All departments and schools have large research programs. As part of the research activity, college personnel hold the primary responsibility for the day-to-day management of the Ontario Ministry of Agriculture and Food (OMAF) research stations at Arkell, Elora, Cambridge, Guelph and Woodstock.

In 1982-83 OAC had 190 full-time professional staff. Of these, 129 taught, fifty-seven conducted research supported by OMAF and fourteen did extension for OMAF. There were 1,876 undergraduate degree students, 400 graduate students and 600 non-academic and part-time support staff. The operating budget of the College was $24.4 million during 1981-82. The Government of Ontario provided $17.9 million of which some $8 million was for research. A further $6.5 million was obtained in external funding for research. Of this amount, 50 percent was obtained from federal granting councils, 14 percent from Agriculture Canada and other federal departments, 10 percent from industry, 17 percent from non-profit organizations and 9 percent from other sources.

For non-OMAF research, decisions on specific research projects are made after discussion between the researcher and the funding agents with approval by the department chairman, the College dean and the Dean of Research. For OMAF funding, the research is divided into program areas (e.g., Beef Research) and the thrust of the program is agreed to by the researchers, the coordinator for the program, the College dean, Dean of Research and the Ontario Ministry of Agriculture and Food. Following this, specific project outlines consistent with the thrust of the program are prepared by the researcher. These projects may have a life of up to three years and project reports are required annually. Major changes in research programs usually take place only after discussion with the Agricultural Research Institute of Ontario.

The Ontario Agricultural Services Coordinating Committee (OASCC), of which the dean is a member, and the network of OASCC committees, to which senior staff members belong, assure additional advice and consultation with regard to research needs and priorities.

Ontario Veterinary College (OVC)

The College was established in 1862 and was part of the Ontario Department of Agriculture until 1965 when it became a college of the University of Guelph. Research probably began soon after establishment and, certainly, in the early 1900s the OVC was contributing significantly to veterinary research. After 1965 the Veterinary Services Branch of OMAF assumed responsibility for essentially all service and consultation, with the OVC being responsible only for research under contract with the Ministry.

Most of the research is in four general areas: reproduction, respiratory problems, digestive problems and problems associated with herd health. Interdisciplinary and cooperative research is emphasized by OVC. Particularly strong research associations are maintained with the Department of Animal and Poultry Science of OAC and the Animal Disease Research Institute of Agriculture Canada in Ottawa.

In 1982-83 the College had a teaching and research staff of 108, 477 undergraduate students and 105 graduate and postgraduate students. The College had twenty-five professional person-years devoted to research. About eighteen were involved with OMAF contracts and about seven person-years were supported by the Ontario Ministry of Colleges and Universities. The total research budget is about $5 million per year, 50 percent from OMAF contracts, 40 percent from granting agencies (including NSERC, Medical Research Council (MRC), Agriculture Canada, Wintario funds, industry and Ontario Ministry of Colleges and Universities) and 10 percent from graduate student personal stipends.

There are basically two mechanisms used to set research priorities. One is through the Ontario Agricultural Services Coordinating Committee (OASCC) of which the dean is a member. It has animal commodity subcommittees, which include practicing veterinarians, and which identify major disease problems affecting production of food animals. These inputs are used by the faculty in establishing research priorities with OMAF contract funding. The second mechanism relates to granting and contracting agencies. Here faculty members, alone or as groups, apply for support to conduct research on a wide range of subjects. Frequently OMAF funding is "topped-up" by grant and contract funds.

MCGILL UNIVERSITY

The agricultural research is conducted at Macdonald College located on Macdonald campus at Ste. Anne de Bellevue, thirty-two kilometres west of Montreal, Quebec. The college was started in 1905 as the result of a donation of land and a $2 million endowment to McGill University by Sir William Macdonald. It was an enlargement of an earlier program organized by Sir William to improve rural education and the training of women for housekeeping and homemaking. Research commenced soon after the College received the first students in 1907. Early research emphasized development of cultivars and production methods for cereals and forages and nutritional requirements for animals.

The College now has departments of Agricultural Chemistry and Physics, Agricultural Economics, Agricultural Engineering, Animal Science, Entomology, Microbiology, Plant Science, Renewable Resources and a school of Food Science. The large departments of Animal Science, Plant Science, Agricultural Engineering and Renewable Resources seem to set the tone for agricultural research of an applied nature, whereas Microbiology, Entomology, Physics and Chemistry tend to have research programs on biological or environmental issues. Agricultural Economics and the School of Food Science have limited, but significant, research programs on a range of agricultural issues. Research is conducted on the campus and at the 230 hectare college farm, the 240 hectare Morgan Arboretum and the 160 hectare Blair Farm project.

During 1982-83 Macdonald College had eighty-one professional academic staff who spent some fifty person-years doing research. They had 780 undergraduate degree students and 210 graduate students. It is estimated that the graduate students provided from 120 to 130 person-years of research and research support. The operating budget of the College for 1981-82 was $4.4 million. The College received an additional $3.3 million of outside funding for research. The Federal Government provided 40 percent of this funding, the province 21 percent, industry 16 percent and international sources 23 percent.

Cooperation with McGill University and with other agricultural research institutes in Quebec is well developed and is encouraged through several provincial councils for research coordination. The senior council is the Quebec Agricultural Research and Services Council, of which the dean is a member. Priorities for research are established by these councils and they promote scientific interaction among the various research units. Within this broad framework, research at Macdonald College is the responsibility of individuals and teams. Since researchers must obtain their funds externally, the research priorities are really set by the granting agencies. Approval of projects for submission for funding involves obtaining the signatures of the Department Chairman, the Associate Dean - Research (Agriculture) and the Vice-Principal (Research), McGill.

UNIVERSITÉ DE MONTRÉAL

Agricultural research at the Université de Montréal is conducted by their Faculté de Médecine Vétérinaire at Saint-Hyacinthe, located forty kilometres east of Montreal. The Faculté was established by the Province in 1886 as a veterinary school. From 1895 to 1920 it was a school of Medicine and Veterinary Science. In 1920 it was one of the founding faculties of the Université de Montréal, but in 1928 returned to provincial affiliation and was moved to Oka where it operated until 1947 when it was moved to its present location. Here it operated under provincial jurisdiction until 1968 when it again affiliated with the Université de Montréal. Until this affiliation, there was little research undertaken.

There are now strong research programs in reproductive physiology, infectious diseases, biomedicine and edible animal by-products. The research is conducted by the fifty academic staff with the assistance of some of the 272 undergraduate students and forty-five graduate students. Financial support of research from all sources was over $1.5 million in 1982. The Province of Quebec provided 43 percent of the funding, the Government of Canada 44 percent, the Université de Montréal 4 percent, other organizations 1 percent and private individuals 8 percent.

In the research there is a strong association with the Université de Montréal, the Province, Agriculture Canada and industry. External coordination and direction is provided by the dean being a member of the Quebec Agricultural Services Coordinating Council (QASCC).

UNIVERSITÉ LAVAL

The agricultural research is conducted by the Faculty of Agriculture. The Faculty was formed in 1962 by moving the colleges of Agriculture at Oka and Ste. Anne de la Pocatière to the campus of Laval in Quebec City. Research with crops, soils and animals that was underway at those locations was brought to Laval and immediately strengthened by employing a number of highly qualified professionals, several from Agriculture Canada.

The Faculty now has departments of Agricultural Economics, Agricultural Engineering, Animal Science, Soil Science, Food Science, Plant Science and Human Nutrition. All departments have developed strong research programs. Jointly with the Research Centre for Nutrition, a research program has been developed in both human and animal nutrition. The Faculty does research on fifteen hectares of land on the campus, thirty-five hectares of land at St. Louis de Pentendre and 350 hectares at St. Augustine. It also does research with fur-bearing animals at Baie St. Paul.

The Faculty had an academic staff of seventy during the 1982-83 fiscal year. It is estimated that 80 percent of the staff did research. There were 915 undergraduate degree students and 174 graduate students, most of whom did research. The research budget for 1982-83 was $2.9 million of which $0.9 million was money carried forward from 1981-82. The Province of Quebec provided 50 percent of the $2 million received for research during 1982-83. Agriculture Canada and NSERC provided 38 percent, other federal agencies 2 percent, the university 3 percent and industry 1 percent.

In the research there is strong association with other faculties at Laval, the Province, Agriculture Canada and industry. The association with Agriculture Canada is aided by having a research station on the campus. Cooperation with Laval and other agricultural research institutes is encouraged and coordinated through several councils for research coordination. The senior committee is the Quebec Agricultural Research and Services Council, of which the dean is a member.

NOVA SCOTIA AGRICULTURAL COLLEGE (NSAC)

The College was started in Truro in 1905 but did not develop degree granting status until 1982. Although the degree program is recent and there is no graduate program, the College has a research program that emphasizes soil and climatic problems associated with the production of livestock, cereal, forage and horticultural crops in the Atlantic provinces. The research with blueberries and fiddlehead ferns is unique.

During 1982-83 the College had a teaching staff of fifty and 219 degree students. The college normally devotes six professional person-years to research. In 1982-83 external funding of research totalled $306 thousand. The Nova Scotia Department of Agriculture & Marketing (NSDA&M) provided 55 percent of the funds, NSERC and NRC 24 percent, Agriculture Canada 13% and industry 8 percent of the funds.

Research is guided by a nine-member research committee established by NSDA&M in 1969. The chairman and three members are senior NSAC faculty. The principal of the College is a member of the Atlantic Agricultural Services Coordinating Committee (AASCC) and senior members of the staff are members of subcommittees and thus are involved in establishing research priorities for the whole Atlantic region.

THE INDUSTRY COMPONENT

There are estimated to be 300 professionals in industry doing agricultural research and development (R&D). On this basis, it is assumed that 15 percent of the agricultural research in Canada is done by industry. This research and development is essentially product and promotion orientated, fragmented among a large number of companies and often inaccessible. Thus, by its very nature, it is virtually impossible to describe in a comprehensive manner.

While it is not possible to describe the whole industry component, it is possible to describe a very significant part — food R&D. The description is based on studies commissioned by the Canadian Agricultural Research Council and discussed at a recent food R&D seminar in Ottawa. The base is 1980 but the values are considered to be essentially valid today.

The Canadian food industry spent $25.8 million on R&D in 1980. The amount spent by individual companies ranged from $1,200 to $5.4 million. Some 80 percent of the R&D was performed by fifteen companies each with an R&D budget in excess of $0.5 million. In 1980 the Canadian food industry employed 794 people in R&D of which 467 were considered to be professionals with B.Sc. (325), M.Sc. (85) or Ph.D. (57) degrees. Since this number exceeds by some 50 percent the number of professionals thought to be doing research in industry, there are obviously classification problems. Regardless, the R&D in the food segment of the agriculture industry will give you an impression of the R&D in the whole agricultural industry.

There is another group of R&D performers that I prefer to associate with industry even though they may not have significant industry financing. I cannot describe them fully but they are typified by the POS Pilot Plant Corporation in Saskatoon and the Canadian Food Products Development Centre in Portage la Prairie. They essentially perform contract research for governments and industry on a fee-for-service basis. During 1980 they are reported to have spent $2.7 million on food research.

And finally, there are a large number of commodity, producer, processor and trade associations that fund some research and sometimes manage funds for others. Most important they tend to act as the conscience of the Canadian Agricultural Research Institution and to have considerable influence on the distribution of research funds. Examples of these are the Canadian Horticultural Council, the Canola Council of Canada, the Brewing and Malting Barley Research Institute, the Canada Grains Council and the newly-formed Western Grains Research Foundation.

COORDINATION

Coordination of the Canadian Agricultural Research Institution, with all of its authorities and complexities, is very difficult. But, there is coordination, often imperfect in detail, but effective in that it gives the general sense of direction that is required. Much of the coordination of detail is done by the association of individuals. The general direction is largely provided by the Canadian Agricultural Services Coordinating Committee and by the Canadian Agricultural Research Council. Both have been referred to during this presentation. I will describe them here.

CANADIAN AGRICULTURAL SERVICES COORDINATING COMMITTEE (CASCC)

The Canadian Agricultural Services Coordinating Committee was established in 1932. It is the federal-provincial coordinating mechanism for agricultural services, including R&D. CASCC considers the recommendations of its provincial or regional counterparts, its special committees and the Canadian Agricultural Research Council. CASCC may recommend action by one or more of the agencies represented by its thirty-six members.

CASCC is responsible only to itself. Each member makes decisions and recommendations in light of the collective judgement of CASCC. Membership includes: provincial deputy ministers; deans of colleges of Agriculture and colleges of Veterinary Medicine; Assistant Deputy Minister, Education, Research and Special Services Division, Ontario Ministry of Agriculture and Food; Chairman, Council of Research and Agricultural Services, Quebec Ministry of Agriculture; the Agricultural Institute of Canada; National Research Council; Statistics Canada, the Agricultural Economics Research Council; and the Deputy Minister and principal officers of Agriculture Canada.

In the Atlantic region, and in each of the other provinces, CASCC has fostered the establishment of a provincial agricultural services coordinating committee. In a province, research managers from each research establishment, whether federal, university or other agencies, are members. Their recommendations, and those from specialist committees, become the business of the coordinating body of a province or region. Recommendations may be forwarded to CASCC or may stimulate action in a province.

CANADIAN AGRICULTURAL RESEARCH COUNCIL (CARC)

The Canadian Agricultural Research Council was established by CASCC in 1974. It had been concluded that development and coordination of Canada's research effort, in support of agricultural and food production, had matured to the stage where it could benefit by advice and guidance from a body representing federal and provincial departments as well as universities, industry and farmers' organizations. Formation was supported by two reports; namely, Science Council's Special Study 10, 1970, entitled "Agricultural Science in Canada," and Science Council's Report 12, 1972, entitled "Two Blades of Grass - The Challenge Facing Agriculture."

CARC is responsible for giving leadership to coordination of the National Agricultural Research program, for advising on research needs, adequacies and priorities, and for recommendations on how to coordinate agricultural research thrusts with policy aims. It recommends priorities in allocation of resources. It makes the national program understood by all.

CARC has nineteen members representing the Science Council of Canada, Le Conseil de Recherche et Services Agricoles du Québec, the Canadian Veterinary Medical Association, the National Research Council, the Canadian Federation of Agriculture, Agriculture Canada, the Association of Faculties of Veterinary Medicine in Canada, the Manitoba Department of Agriculture, the Alberta Agricultural Services Coordinating Committee, the British Columbia Agricultural Services Coordinating Committee, the Association of Faculties of Agriculture in Canada, the Atlantic Provinces Agricultural Services Coordinating Committee, the Agricultural Institute of Canada, the Canadian Chamber of Commerce, the Ontario Agricultural Services Coordinating Committee, the Ministry of State for Science and Technology, the deans of Agriculture and Veterinary Medicine, the

National Farmer's Union and the Saskatchewan Agricultural Services Coordinating Committee.

CARC emphasizes the national needs of agricultural R&D. Six Canada Committees, responsible to CASCC, make recommendations through CARC. They are the Canada Committee on Agricultural Engineering Services, Canada Committee on Animal Production Services, Canada Committee on Crop Production Services, Canada Committee on Food, Canada Committee on Land Resource Services and Canada Committee on Socio-Economic Services. There is also the Canada Committee on International Agricultural Services. There are twenty-three expert committees under the Canada committees.

The Research Branch of Agriculture Canada provides the Secretariat and finances the operation of CASCC and CARC. It also maintains on a computer the Inventory of Canadian Agricultural Research (ICAR) developed by CARC.

CONCLUDING COMMENTS

The Canadian Agricultural Research Institution has developed well during the past 100 years. It has developed on the basis of need and has had strong support by governments. It has played a significant role in the development of an agricultural industry that is efficient, except when there are extreme deviations in production environment, transport capability or market demand. It is respected nationally and internationally.

With present attitudes and levels of funding, many of us are concerned for the sustainability of the Institution. We do not believe that it will disappear, but fear that it will be so reduced in effectiveness that it will not properly serve the industry. The physical structure is still here but the operational efficiency is declining.

This is happening because the importance of the agricultural industry and the need for research to sustain the industry is not understood by the majority of the public. With ample food on the supermarket shelf, there is little need for the public to learn or to be concerned. This attitude is reflected by governments, except for those in provinces that are largely agricultural. There appears to be little prospect for improvement.

Obviously, the public must be instructed. They must be told of the importance of research and of the value of research to the industry and the consumer. Our problem is that we really do not know the value of research sufficiently well to describe it in simple, straightforward, believable terms. We must learn the value before we start to talk to the public.

SOURCES OF INFORMATION

Most information was received from correspondence and conversation with those listed below. Many provided reports that were used but are not listed. A few other reports were used as references and these are listed. The Inventory of Canadian Agricultural Research, 1980, prepared by CARC, was used extensively as a general reference.

Development

Future Thrusts - Research and Development for Canada's Agriculture and Food System. Canadian Agricultural Council, December 1981.

- - Evaluation of Research and Development in Agriculture and Food in Canada. A Report presented to the Canadian Agricultural Research Council by D.G. Hamilton, January 15, 1980.
- - Agricultural Research in Western Canada. Prepared by J.E.R. Greenshields and R.K. Downey for the Canada West Foundation, 245 West Palliser Square, Calgary.

Federal

Research Branch - Dr. E.J. LeRoux, Assistant Deputy Minister, Research; Dr. R.L. Halstead, Director General, Planning and Evaluation; Dr. J.R. Aitken, Contracts Analyst; and Drs. C.J. Bishop and W.J. Saidak, Program Coordinators, Research Branch, Ottawa.

Animal Pathology Division - Dr. N.G. Willis, Director, Animal Pathology Division, Health of Animals Directorate, Food Production and Inspection Branch, Agriculture Canada, Ottawa.

Grain Research Laboratory - Dr. K.H. Tipples, Director, and Dr. G.E. LaBerge, Research Scientist, Grain Research Laboratory, Canadian Grain Commission, Winnipeg.

National Research Council - Dr. W. Steck, Divisional Director, Plant Biotechnology Institute, National Research Council, Saskatoon.

Provincial

British Columbia - Dr. G.A. MacEachern, A/Deputy Minister and W.W. Wiebe, Director, Field and Special Crops Branch, British Columbia Ministry of Agriculture and Food, Victoria.

Alberta - H.B. McEwan, Deputy Minister and Dr. A.O. Olson, Assistant Deputy Minister, Research and Resource Development, Alberta Agriculture, Edmonton.

Saskatchewan - J.L. Drew, Deputy Minister, Saskatchewan Department of Agriculture, Regina.

Manitoba - T.L. Pringle, Assistant Deputy Minister, Agricultural Development and Marketing, Manitoba Agriculture, Winnipeg.

Ontario - Dr. J.C. Rennie, Assistant Deputy Minister, Technology and Field Services, Ontario Ministry of Agriculture and Food, Toronto.

Quebec - Ferdinand Ouellet, Deputy Minister and Fernand Gauthier, Director General, Québec Ministère de L'Agriculture des Pêcheries et l'Alimentation, Quebec.

New Brunswick - J.T.G. Andrew, Deputy Minister, New Brunswick Department of Agriculture and Rural Development, Fredericton.

Nova Scotia - W.V. Grant, Deputy Minister, Nova Scotia Department of Agriculture and Marketing, Halifax and Dr. H.F. MacRae, Principal, Nova Scotia Agricultural College, Truro.

Prince Edward Island - H. Lloyd Palmer, Deputy Minister, Department of Agriculture and Forestry, Charlottetown.

Newfoundland and Labrador - G.J. O'Reilly, Deputy Minister, Department of Rural, Agricultural and Northern Development, St. John's.

Universities

British Columbia - Dr. W.D. Kitts, Dean, Faculty of Agricultural Sciences, Vancouver.

Alberta - Dr. J.P. Bowland, Dean, Faculty of Agriculture and Forestry, Edmonton.

Saskatchewan - Dr. G.E. Lee, Associate Dean (Research), College of Agriculture, Saskatoon.

- Dr. G.F. Hamilton, Dean and Dr. R.L. Polley, Assistant Dean, Western College of Veterinary Medicine, Saskatoon.

Manitoba - Dr. R.C. McGinnis, Dean, and L.B. Siemens, Associate Dean, Faculty of Agriculture, Winnipeg.

Guelph - Dr. C.M. Switzer, Dean, Ontario Agricultural College, Guelph.

- Dr. R.A. Willoughby, Associate Dean, Ontario Veterinary College, Guelph.

McGill - Dr. A.F. MacKenzie, Associate Dean, Research, Macdonald College, Ste. Anne de Bellevue.

Montreal - Dr. Raymond S. Roy, Doyen, Faculté de Médecine Vétérinaire, Saint-Hyacinthe.

Laval - Dr. M. Trudel, Doyen, Faculté des Sciences de l'Agriculture et de l'Alimentation, Quebec.

Nova Scotia - Dr. H.F. MacRae, Principal, Nova Scotia Agricultural College, Truro.

Industry

Proceedings of the Food R&D Seminar, 19-20 April 1983, Agriculture Canada, Ottawa.

Coordination

Canadian Agricultural Services Coordinating Committee (CASCC), Role and Organization, April 1982.

- Canadian Agricultural Research Council, Annual Report, January 1983.

THEORETICAL ISSUES IN
RESEARCH EVALUATION

CHAPTER 4

AN ANALYSIS OF PUBLIC AGRICULTURAL RESEARCH IN THE CANADIAN PRAIRIE PROVINCES

H. G. Brooks and W. H. Furtan

INTRODUCTION

The role of the public in producing agricultural research output and innovations has been under close scrutiny for the past decade. The change in public opinion concerning the benefits of public agricultural research has been precipitated by externalities and distributional effects resulting from technical change.

At present the research sector in Canadian agriculture is largely unexplained with respect to how the level of funds to agriculture and within (between) agricultural commodities is determined. The realization by all participants of the agricultural sector that the decisions made by the public sector on allocation of research expenditures affects them directly leads to competition for research funds.

This paper develops a conceptual model of the Canadian agricultural research sector to explain the allocation of public expenditures on commodity specific research. The model is specified and tested using data on university research expenditures in the Canadian prairie provinces to determine the significant variables affecting the pattern of agricultural research among commodity groups. The policy implications that result from the estimated relationships are examined.

The increases in Canadian and world food production has in part been generated by agricultural research output. The importance of public funding in the Canadian agricultural research sector is large, as can be seen in Table 1. The rationale supporting this overwhelming influence of government involvement are that:

1) In many cases the private rate of return (capturable returns) from investment in research provides inadequate incentives to private investors, while the social returns to agricultural research have been documented as being significantly higher than the market rate of return.

2) The process of agricultural research is obviously complementary with the educational institutions and, thus, has cost advantages over the private non-educational institutions.

3) Public agricultural research may maintain the competitive structures in agricultural input supply firms and marketing firms.

With the premise accepted by many that the public sector has a justifiable role to play in agricultural research, the question becomes how the level of investment in agricultural commodities should be determined. Public interest theory dictates that the government will invest in research until the costs (expenditures and opportunity costs) are equated to the present value of the future stream of research benefits. This theory views the demand curve for agricultural research as the marginal social cost of research. If the market operates efficiently, it will generate an equilibrium consistent with the public interest.

An alternative approach to explaining the agricultural research sector is through the theory of economic regulation. This theory was developed to "explain who will receive the benefits or burdens of regulation, what form regulation will take,

TABLE 1

BREAKDOWN OF AGRICULTURAL RESEARCH EFFORT IN PROVINCES
AS A PERCENTAGE OF PROFESSIONAL PERSON-YEARS

	Federal	Provincial-University	Industry
Newfoundland	84	16	0
Nova Scotia	71	14	11
Prince Edward Island	100	0	0
New Brunswick	96	0.5	3
Quebec	28	44	27
Ontario	19	49	31
Manitoba	56	40	4
Saskatchewan	50	35	10
Alberta	51	39	9
British Columbia	40	40	18

Source: Hamilton, 1980, p. 31.

and the effect of regulation upon the allocation of resources'' (Stigler, 1971, p. 114). This theory identifies groups which act in a reasonably consistent manner on specific issues of interest to them and the process through which they affect the government on these issues. These ''interest groups'' are formed either implicitly, or explicitly, on how the regulation will improve, or decrease, their net welfare position.

The first part of this paper reviews the institutional arrangements of agricultural research in Canada. The second section specifies a supply and demand curve for agricultural research, while the empirical part of the paper deals with agricultural research in the prairie region of Canada. Conclusions and some policy implications are given in the final section of the paper.

INSTITUTIONAL STRUCTURES IN
AGRICULTURAL RESEARCH IN CANADA

The Canadian research sector can be viewed in Figure 1. The research supply institutions are represented by the provincial departments of Agriculture, Agriculture Canada, the universities' faculties of Agriculture, and a small amount of industry research. The breakdown on research effort in 1977 (in terms of professional man-years) is: federal, approximately 60 percent; provincial, approximately 5 percent; universities, approximately 28 percent; and industry, approximately 6 percent.

The coordinating bodies established in Canada to monitor and control the research effort are mostly at the federal level. The Canadian Agricultural Services Coordinating Committee (CASCC) (established in 1932) is responsible for the coordination of the total national agricultural research effort in Canada. Its stated objective is to promote the most efficient use of professional and technical

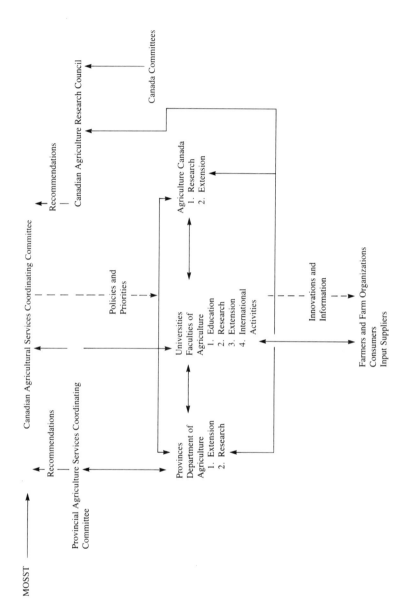

Figure 1
Structure of the Canadian Research System

staff, and the most efficient allocation of finances among and within all research-producing institutions. The CASCC is chaired by the Deputy Minister of Agriculture Canada and its members include provincial deputy ministers of Agriculture, senior provincial and federal research managers, deans of faculties of Agriculture and Veterinary Medicine, and representatives of the National Research Council, Statistics Canada, and the Agriculture Institute of Canada. CASCC is a fully autonomous body that assimilates the recommendations of other groups and forms the national set of policy recommendations and priorities.

The Canadian Agricultural Research Council (CARC) is an autonomous body formed by CASCC in 1974 and has the responsibility of advising the government on the state of agricultural research in Canada and recommending changes to it. It maintains an inventory of agricultural research and development and advises CASCC on the adequacy of R&D in Canada. CARC also advises the CASCC on the R&D recommendations of the provincial and regional agricultural services coordinating committees, the Canada committees, and other sources.

The Agricultural Services Coordinating Committees (ASCCs) are the seven provincial and regional counterparts to CASCC.[1] They were established to coordinate the provincial research effort and make recommendations to the CASCC on research and development.

The Ministry of State for Science and Technology (MOSST) was established in 1971 to advise government on research and development issues with regard to the government's stated socio-economic objectives. Research and development is "one of the main policy instruments employed by Agriculture Canada, and by provincial governments on behalf of the agriculture and food industry" (Hamilton, 1980, p. 21). MOSST formulates national science policies and advises federal departments on priorities.

The Canada committees are established to advise CASCC through CARC on specific areas such as Agricultural Engineering or Animal Production. There are presently seven Canada committees and twenty-three expert committees under them.

The four-equation model used in this study to explain the allocation of research funds in Canada explicitly takes into account the information flow between farmers, research-producing institutions and the research regulatory bodies of government. The model includes a demand relation, supply relation, allocation relation and an identity equation.

DEMAND RELATION FOR COMMODITY SPECIFIC RESEARCH

The demand for agricultural research at the provincial or university research level is specified to be chiefly from farmers or farm groups. The demand at the federal research level (Agriculture Canada) is also hypothesized to be from farmers but this demand operates more through the bureaucratic structures and political system, i.e., MOSST, CARC, CASCC. Obviously, there is a great deal of reinforcement of demand between the research institutions through the coordinating bodies.

The demand relation for agricultural technology is a function of (1) the relative size (number and wealth) of the group that gains from research, (2) the level of organization of the group, (3) the amount of gain the individuals of the interest group expect to receive, and (4) the demand by other interests who would lose directly from the research output.

The relative size of the interest group which gains from the effort can be measured by the number of farm units that they represent, the number of voters they represent (and the marginal product of the votes), and the resources that they have available for a lobbying effort, i.e., the wealth position of these farmers.

The level of organization of the group which will gain from technological change may be a result of other economic factors. If all of the gainers are producers of the same commodity and the commodity group has an existing organization, this should increase their ability to reflect demand. As interest groups do form along commodity lines, this is an important variable. This could be measured as the number of farmers who receive their main source of income from a specific commodity group, the total number of farmers producing the commodity, or all those producers who could possibly go into production of the commodity. The latter more general measure may be discounted because the competitive nature of the agricultural market may bid the Schumpeterian profits away.

The level of gains an individual expects to receive is a function of the form of the technical change, the individual's ability to capitalize the Schumpeterian profits and the individual's ability to incorporate the technical change. The individual's ability to capture the gains depends on his ability to incorporate the technology. This depends on the human capital of the farms units and may be measured as years of on-farm experience, or years of formal education of the farm unit. The ability to incorporate the technology may also depend on the capital required to use the technology. If the capital requirements are large, this may lessen the intensity of demand by smaller farm units and increase the relative demand by larger farmers. (Large farmers could also expect more absolute gains because of their size.)

The level of gains that could be captured by individuals will also depend on whether the producers are the owners of the inelastic inputs, i.e., land base. This allows them to capitalize the Schumpeterian profits created by the innovation.[2] It is expected that the higher the proportion of owner-operators in the interest group, the larger the gains to those individuals and the higher the intensity of demand. The size of gains attributable to the locally applied research product will also depend on the availability of commodity specific applied research from other areas. If technology from other areas is available and transferable to the local production process this would decrease the demand for local research. If the technology is non-transferable, the demand for local research effort may shift to the right, because without the technology the local area loses relative production advantage.

The demand by other interest groups which would lose from the research or which are competing for research funds will be affected by the size of their losses, the size of their groups and the number of groups. If interest groups are very diverse, i.e., many equal-sized interest groups in a sector, it is expected that the amount of research dollars needed to satisfy each interest group would increase. This is specified to be a result of the lack of scale in both lobbying for research and in supplying research.

The demand relation for research will also be price responsive and, because the public good is not traded in the market, this is its shadow price. The shadow value is the opportunity cost of the next best alternative for the funds used. To the individual in the commodity interest groups this would be negatively related to their demand. However, the distributional effects of research output that benefit their interest is large when compared to their incremental share of society's increased tax burden.

Economic stress on the farm units will also lead to an increased intensity of demand. This can be either a result of a shift in relative prices or a general increase in the price level of farm inputs because both will lead to decreased profitability in the short run.

The demand relation for commodity specific applied public research in Canada is postulated as:

$$R_i = f(S_i, SD_i, T_i, E_i, CD, I_i, P_i, B_i) \tag{1}$$

where R_i = the quantity of commodity specific applied research demanded for commodity i,

S_i = the size of total agricultural output in a region,

SD_i = the size distribution of farms producing commodity i,

T_i = the tenure status of farms producing commodity i,

E_i = the education level of farmers producing commodity i,

CD = the commodity diversity of region,

I_i = the agricultural input prices in production of i,

P_i = the shadow value of research, and

B_i = the technology specific to commodity i that is conducted in other areas.

SUPPLY RELATION OF COMMODITY SPECIFIC RESEARCH

Commodity specific applied agricultural research is supplied by the universities, Agriculture Canada and the provincial governments. This output may be in the form of journal articles, technical publications, improved genetic stock (plant or animal), new production formulas and techniques, chemicals to improve growth of agricultural output or any other increase in the stock of scientific knowledge which can be utilized by producers. The research generated by these institutions is typically a public good and is free to any user once it is available.

The production process requires researchers, technicians and assistants, administrators, clinical staff, building space for offices and laboratories, libraries (i.e., stocks of scientific information), plant plots and livestock housing, stocks of plants and animals and specialized scientific equipment. The bulk of these costs are attributed to staff salaries. The contribution of each of these inputs to total cost depends on the scale of the research units.

The supply of research in Canada is certainly affected by the cost of the variable inputs and the supply curve will shift in response to changes in the general price level of inputs. This can be viewed as follows: when research costs rise there are substitution affects (e.g., hire more technicians, universities hire post-doctorate workers, etc. as substitutes for Ph.D. faculty), and income effects (exhibited in the cutback of projects).

The existence of basic or semi-basic research from other areas also affects the production of applied research output. Because applied research is not perfectly transferable, i.e., commodity or geographically specific, areas find it profitable to produce their own research. Producing the indigenous research from a low level of information is very costly and the existence of basic and semi-basic knowledge will greatly reduce the cost. The knowledge may also aid in a source of transferable methodology and research techniques, or in generating new ideas. It is expected that the ''size'' of outside basic and semi-basic knowledge will have a positive relation with the supply of applied commodity specific research.

The supply relation for commodity specific applied agricultural research in Canada is postulated to be as follows:

$$P_i = g(CD, RI_i, RS, D_i, R_i) \tag{2}$$

where P_i = price of commodity i applied research,
  CD = commodity diversity of region,
  RI_i = price of research inputs for commodity i,
  RS = size of borrowable basic and semi-basic research output,
  D_i = managerial ability of research director for commodity i, and
  R_i = the quantity of commodity specific applied research supplied for commodity i.

ALLOCATION RELATION FOR COMMODITY SPECIFIC RESEARCH

The allocation relation for commodity specific applied agricultural research is an institutional and behavioural relation which relates the distribution of research funding and effort. In the Canadian research sector the farmers, land owners and input suppliers do not directly pay the university faculties of Agriculture or Agriculture Canada for the production of new technology. The decisions on levels of funding are made at a high governmental level, by the provincial cabinet for university funding and provincial research, and by the federal cabinet for

Agriculture Canada. A behavioural relation models the interaction of variables that determine the level and distribution of the funds over all the levels of government and research decision makers.

The demand expressed by farmers and other interests is to the suppliers of the research output through two channels. One channel is direct contact, i.e., extension services, meetings, etc., while the other is through the political-bureaucratic channels. The ability of a commodity group to have public funds appropriated for commodity specific applied research is thus a function of its ability to bargain through the political-bureaucratic system. The variables outlined in the theoretical review that affect this ability are the number of farmers (size of the group), the wealth of the group (size of farms), and the relative gains the individuals of the group can expect.

Thus we would expect that as the size of a commodity group increased it would be able to lobby for a larger portion of the agricultural research dollars relative to other groups.

The size of the farm units will also affect their ability to convince the public institutions to increase their technology supply. When the farm units producing a commodity are large or wealthy compared to farm units producing other commodities, we would expect an increase in the government expenditures on research specific to that commodity. This variable may be represented by the income of the commodity group (e.g., the proportion of farmers selling products worth in excess of $25 thousand).

The sales a farm makes each year also represent the individual's ability to gain from technological change in terms of magnitude. If commodity specific applied research leads to per unit cost reductions, a firm with more production and more sales will gain absolutely more than a smaller firm. The size of farms will affect the demand and thus the intensity and success of lobbying efforts of farmers.

The ability of the commodity group to capitalize the gains from technical change into the most inelastic input (most probably land) enhances the size of gains they can accumulate from research. The tenure status of the commodity group measured as the proportion of farms that are owned by the operator (or partially owned) will thus be positively related to the funds allocated to that commodity's applied research.

An obvious determinant of the level of funds allocated to agricultural research is the total expenditure of the government involved. This is an income variable for a normal good; i.e., as public income increases the expenditure on agricultural research increases.

The ability of the research director to allocate funds is also an important variable in this relation. The director will initiate and coordinate the requests of his research staff for commodity specific research, and he controls research activity through the regular budgeting process. The director will have knowledge of the cost of research inputs and the demand by producer groups. He will coordinate the staff and research activity accordingly.

The allocation equation for commodity specific applied agricultural research is thus as follows:

$$RE_i = h(T_i, SD_i, O_i, TE, D_i) \qquad (3)$$

where RE_i = expenditures on commodity specific applied research,
T_i = tenure status of farmers producing commodity i,
SD_i = size distribution of farms producing commodity i,
D_i = managerial ability of research director for commodity i,
O_i = commodity group size and organization, and
TE = total government expenditures.

REDUCED-FORM EQUATION

To empirically estimate the model it is necessary to construct a reduced-form equation of the Canadian Agriculture research sector. This is due to the nature of the dependent and independent variables, which are difficult or impossible to measure objectively. The reduced-form equation is as follows:

$$\ln RE_i = a_1 + b\ln S_i + c\ln I_i + d\ln E_i + e\ln SD_i + f\ln T_i + g\ln TE + h\ln O_i + j\ln RI_i + k\ln CD + \Omega_i \qquad (4)$$

where RE_i = expenditures on commodity i specific applied research,
S = net agricultural output in region,
I_i = price of inputs used to produce commodity i,
E_i = education level of farmers producing commodity i,
SD_i = size distribution of farms producing commodity i,
T_i = tenure structure of farms producing commodity i,
TE = total government expenditures,
O_i = commodity i group organization size,
RI_i = price of research inputs in research of commodity,
CD = commodity diversity of region, and
Ω_i = error term.

The structure of the reduced-form equation allows for estimation of the model in at least a partial manner. The complexity of the expressions in the four-equation model makes it difficult to hypothesize signs for some of the reduced-form coefficients.

The reduced-form equation was specified to hold for the commodity groups: beef, dairy, swine, poultry and eggs, wheat and barley. The time period specified for the testing of the model is the post-World War II era, 1946-1980 (35 observations).

The main constraint to testing the model of agricultural research was the inability to collect any significant data for expenditures on research in a usable form from the federal government research institutions (i.e., Agriculture Canada). The individual research stations are only required to store budgetary information for six years and after this time period the information is destroyed. The inability to include federal government data on expenditures for commodity specific research placed a constraint on our ability to test the model. It was necessary to make the assumption that the mix of research effort on commodity specific applied research carried on by Agriculture Canada was not significantly different from the other research suppliers, i.e., the provincial departments and university faculties of Agriculture.

The next set of institutions with incomplete records were the provincial departments of Agriculture who did not compile information in a usable manner. The provincial research was in some cases funneled through the university system and captured in this manner.[3]

Thus, the only institutional research that was measurable for the 1946-1980 period was for university agricultural research.[4] The budgetary data for the departments in the colleges of Agriculture were available for this time period as well as the structure of the faculties' researchers, the physical plant of the colleges and the research grants that were used by the universities on commodity specific research.

The data that were available at the universities on research expenditures for commodity specific research were in a highly aggregated form. Most data were retrieved from the operating budgets and listed by department in the annual financial reports. The data required for the testing of the model were total research expenditures for the universities aggregated by commodity group and by province for the years 1946-1980. The commodities chosen to test the model were categorized as beef, dairy, poultry, swine, wheat and barley. To represent the effort of commodity specific applied research the assumption was made that the departments of Animal Science conducted all the applied production research on animals and the departments of Plant (Crop) Science conducted all this effort on the cereal crops.

The disaggregation of the department budgets and grants and contracts into expenditure figures for research into these six commodity classes required further restricting assumptions. To disaggregate the yearly budgets it was necessary to assume that each researcher used approximately the same resources and energy from the departmental sources. This assumption allowed for the disaggregation of the budgets through the faculty person-years that were specialized in the specific commodities research.[5] The index of person-year research effort that was derived for the universities was also used to determine the building space attributable to each commodity where the buildings were multi-purpose (e.g., general animal science office space as opposed to dairy barns). The cost of the building was determined by the original cost, maintenance cost and salvage value. These were used to determine a rental cost that was added to the salary cost of researchers and grants to give a total yearly figure for expenditures on the six commodities at a university.[6]

These calculations were carried out for the University of Manitoba (Animal Science and Plant Science departments) and the University of Saskatchewan (Animal Science and Plant Science departments) because the relevant data could be collected from stored annual budgets, annual reports and the descriptive help of senior faculty members. The University of Alberta, however, has complete data for the 1970-1980 period only.[7] The incompleteness of the Alberta data could in no way be overcome and thus the final series of commodity specific research expenditures consisted of the following:

University of Saskatchewan: Total Expenditure Data 1946-1980,

University of Manitoba: Total Expenditure Data 1946-1980.

The independent variables used in equation 4 are described in Table 2.

TABLE 2

SUMMARY STATISTICS FOR EMPIRICAL TEST OF MODEL OF CANADIAN AGRICULTURAL RESEARCH SECTOR

Variables	Symbol	Units	Saskatchewan		Manitoba	
			Mean	St. Dev.	Mean	St. Dev.
Wheat Research Exp. at Universities	REW	ln('000s)	8.559	.676	8.484	.400
University Barley Research Expenditures	RE_{BAR}	``	4.878	2.579	7.483	.538
University Beef Research Expenditures	RE_B	``	6.193	3.272	8.643	.690
University Dairy Research Expenditures	RE_D	``	7.224	.843	8.394	.718
University Swine Research Expenditures	RE_S	``	8.479	.238	8.222	1.058
University Poultry Research Expenditures	RE_P	``	8.464	.115	10.831	2.083
Size of Agricultural Output (Net Farm Income)	S_i	(000,000s)	552.469	364.884	175.743	97.557
Ave. Wage of Hired Male Farm Labour	I_i	($)	1.833	1.281	1.767	1.279
Size Distribution of Farms	SD_i	%	.114	.099	.087	.087
Proportion Owner-Operators	T_i	%	71.149	2.31	77.758	2.042
Index of Farmers' Education	E_i		.220	.095	.220	.095
Number of Farmers Producing Commodity	O_i					
Wheat	O_w	('000s)	43.325	6.50	10.125	4.901
Barley	O_{BAR}	``	9.268	1.968	7.733	.835
Beef	O_B	``	6.538	2.231	4.55	1.102
Dairy	O_D	``	.833	.202	1.57	.284
Swine	O_S	``	.824	.201	1.007	.484
Poultry	O_P	``	.221	.052	.470	.164
Index of Associate Professor's Salary	RI_i	('000s)	13.215	8.697	13.215	8.697
Index of Commodity Diversity	CD	.403	.077	.571	.091	

TABLE 3

ORDINARY LEAST SQUARES ESTIMATES OF REDUCED-FORM EQUATION ON PUBLIC EXPENDITURES ON COMMODITY SPECIFIC UNIVERSITY RESEARCH ON THE PRAIRIE PROVINCES

ln(RE)	Man. Crop Research	Sask. Crop Research	Sask.-Man. Beef Research	Sask.-Man. Dairy Research	Sask.-Man. Swine Research	Sask.-Man. Poultry Research
Constant	32.301 (3.27)	47.197 (6.13)	-31.48 (-3.09)	9.195 (.57)	-.396 (-.03)	-23.33 (-1.95)
ln(S)	-.084 (-1.54)	-0.53 (-.76)	.043 (.69)	.009 (.12)	-.067 (-.79)	.120 (1.33)
ln(I_i)	-.466 (-1.08)	1.127 (2.24)	-.448 (-1.05)	.069 (.13)	.621 (1.06)	-1.643 (-2.68)
ln(E_i)	-1.119 (-5.53)	.222 (1.17)	-.537 (-1.93)	-.211 (-.67)	.437 (1.67)	-.576 (-1.52)
ln(SD_i)	.298 (2.52)	-.033 (-.14)	.625 (3.49)	.305 (1.25)	.321 (1.39)	.805 (.315)
ln(T_i)	-5.37 (-2.64)	-7.314 (-4.40)	8.360 (3.98)	-.75 (-.22)	2.717 (1.08)	6.358 (2.47)
ln(TE)	1.172 (6.52)	.693 (1.96)	.752 (2.64)	.81 (2.20)	.195 (.49)	1.325 (2.99)
ln(O_i)	-.545 (-.307)	-1.378 (-4.46)	.322 (.78)	-1.01 (-2.77)	.138 (.65)	.180 (.69)
ln(RI_i)	-1.216 (-2.47)	-1.259 (-2.28)	.890 (1.66)	.485 (.69)	.090 (.13)	.191 (.26)
ln(CD)	.051 (.18)	.294 (1.77)	.253 (1.67)	-.056 (-.21)	.267 (1.18)	.371 (1.38)
$\overline{R}^2$	.97	.94	.99	.98	.98	.98
R^2	.97	.92	.99	.98	.98	.98
D.W.	1.45	1.33	1.65	1.503	.921	1.456
d.f.	25	25	25	25	25	25
Equation No.	1	2	3	4	5	6

The student "t" values are in parentheses.

ESTIMATION

The results of the empirical estimation are presented in Table 3. Equations 1 and 2 test the reduced-form equation for Manitoba crop research (wheat and barley) and Saskatchewan crop research, respectively. Equations 3 to 6 test the model for the livestock commodity classes using the aggregated Saskatchewan-Manitoba data.

The ability of the reduced-form expenditure equation to explain the total variation in the research expenditures is interesting and the significance of some of the variables is also promising.

The positive hypothesized relation for the coefficient on the size of agricultural output (S_i) is not supported by the empirical estimation. The null hypothesis, that the expenditures on the research groups is not a relation of the size of total agricultural output, is found.

The coefficients estimated on the index of farm input costs (average wages of hired farm labour) are conflicting. The positive hypothesized relation is found to be significant in the Saskatchewan crop research equation. A significant negative relation is found for Saskatchewan-Manitoba Poultry specific research and in all other equations it is not significantly different from zero.

The variable approximating farmers' education (E_i) was estimated to be generally significantly negative or not different from zero. This supports the findings of Huffman and Miranowski (1981) and indicates that farmers' education may substitute for public commodity specific research. The increased education may allow them to more fully incorporate and borrow existing research.

The coefficient for the size distribution of farms (SD_i) was estimated to be generally positive as was a priori hypothesized. This provides limited support for the hypothesis that larger and wealthier farmers are able to influence the expenditures of public monies through the allocation equation and demand equation.

The coefficient on the tenure status variable (T_i) was generally estimated to be significantly negative for the crop research equations and significantly positive for the livestock research equations. The a priori sign hypothesized was positive because farmers with full or partial land ownership are able to capture more of the gains from technical innovation. The negative relation for the crop equations may indicate that the ownership of land in crop production (which is more land extensive than livestock production) provided a protective barrier against the economic stress of input cost increase and price decrease, and/or that land generally rose in value (specifically after 1972) and there was less economic stress on crop farmers and thus less demand for research.

The coefficient on the government expenditure variable was estimated as significantly positive in most equations. This supports the hypothesis that because government is spending greater amounts of money, it will spend more on agricultural research. This supports the findings of Peterson (1969) and Huffman and Miranowski (1981).

The estimated coefficient for farm organizations, i.e., number of farmers producing the commodity, was generally significantly negative. This contradicts the a priori hypothesized positive relation. This is possibly because the general exodus of population, decreased number of farms and decreased number of farmers was not taken into account in the variable. This may indicate that as farmers producing the commodities decreased, their wealth increased and also their ability to lobby for research funds.

The coefficient on the cost of research inputs variable was estimated to be significantly negative or not different from zero. This provides limited support for the hypothesis that as the cost of producing research output increases the public will supply less, i.e., the supply of research is price responsive.

The commodity diversity variable was largely insignificant over the time period estimated. This indicates that the increased diversity of agricultural production in the prairies (as measured by sum of squared product shares) has no effect on the research expenditures on the crop sector.

POLICY IMPLICATIONS

The policy implications that derive from the estimation of the reduced-form equation rest on the performance of the equations and the structure of the four-equation model. The strongest relationships evident in this set of equations are in the variables for farmers' education, farm size distribution and total government expenditures. As mentioned in the previous sections, the education variable has a significant negative relationship with the commodity specific research expenditures while the farm size distribution and total government expenditure variables show a significant positive relationship with research expenditures.

The discussion of policy implications proceeds from the specification of farmers' education as a demand equation variable, government expenditures as an allocation equation variable, and farm size distribution as both a demand and allocation equation variable.

The implications resulting from the negative relationship between farmers' education and the demand for agricultural research are intriguing. This relationship is hypothesized to result from an increase in farmers' ability to borrow and adapt commodity specific research. Farmers may be performing their own private search for innovations as their education increases and modifying it to their unique conditions. This is consistent with results obtained by Huffman and Miranowski (1981). This result indicates that as farmers become more educated the extension services of the research institutions can be refocused to serve them more efficiently. Farmers may wish for more information on technology being developed in competing regions or countries and adopting this rather than developing it in their home region. When considering the relative importance of the United States agricultural market and research institutions to the Canadian agricultural sector, it is not surprising that Canadian producers may be borrowing research rather than demanding it of the public research sector.

The positive relation established between government expenditures (as a proxy for government wealth) and research expenditures indicates that wealthier areas are likely to have more effort on agricultural research. This may indicate that farmers in relatively poor regions will receive less research output and may lose in terms of comparative advantage relative to producers in wealthier regions (all else held constant). This effect could perhaps be compensated for by the federal research institutions as an active policy of equalization of agriculturally produced wealth.

The positive coefficient on the size distribution of farms, i.e., proportion of farms that are large, indicates a positive effect through two mechanisms. The relationship implies that large farmers may perceive that they will receive more benefits from agricultural research and thus their demand intensity is larger than small farmers. As well, the large farmers may be more effective lobbyists for agricultural research because of wealth differences. This may indicate to public research institutions that they are responding to a biased sample of demand for research output. This is especially true if the research demanded by large farmers is different from that demanded by small farmers. This type of relation was found by De Janvry (1973) to exist in the case of Argentinian agriculture. If closer examination of the research sector finds this to be the case, the agricultural research sector could react to compensate for the smaller farmer's inability to adequately express his demands for innovations. With the significant trend to increasingly larger farm size this will conceivably be more important in future years.

SUMMARY

This study has developed a four-equation model of agricultural research in Canada using some aspects of special interest theory, institutional theory and economic variables. The demand, supply and allocation equations were developed with special reference to the Canadian agricultural research sector and the more restrictive prairie agricultural research sector. The conceptual model developed is designed to explain the allocation of public expenditures on commodity specific applied research. The reduced-form equation of the model was estimated for six commodity classes (two crops, four livestock groups) to test the applicability of the model over the commodity groups.

The evaluation of the reduced-form equation model and the implications that derive from it give an interesting view of the Canadian research sector. Some variables did perform as *a priori* expected with relative consistency and certain equations performed very well. These results did lead to some implications for the Canadian agricultural research sector.

The general performance of the reduced-form equation and its ability to explain the total variation of expenditures on commodity specific agricultural research gives limited support to the model developed. The results tend to indicate that agricultural research is responsive to economic and institutional variables.

NOTES

1. The ASCCs are as follows: Atlantic Provinces ASCC, Quebec ARSC, Ontario ASCC, Manitoba ASCC, Saskatchewan ASCC, Alberta ASCC, British Columbia ASCC.

2. This is also a function of the nature of the technical change. If the innovation substitutes for land or complements land, it will have an effect on the size of gains to owners of land.

3. Examples of provincial funding being channeled through the university budgets are the Glenlea Research Station in Manitoba and the Crop Development Centre in Saskatchewan.

4. The institutional constraints on the data were key not only to the restriction of the study to university research but also to the restriction of the study to the prairie provinces. With only university research observable, the prairie provinces of Alberta, Saskatchewan and Manitoba form an area of fairly similar agricultural production and technology. To restrict the study to this area, the assumption that the inward and outward flows of technology were comparable had to be made.

5. The specialization of the faculty members was derived through discussions with long-time faculty members, references to the faculty's publications in the years, grants for specific research received by the faculty members in the years and work carried out by graduate students or the faculty members. This was done for the years 1946-1975. For the years 1976-1980 the Inventory of Canadian Agricultural Research (ICAR) was used to determine the specialities of faculty members in university Animal Science and Plant Science departments.

6. The rental rate was derived by the formula $C_n = I/Y \ (1+r)^n + m$ where C_n = rental cost in the nth year, I = initial cost, Y = life of structure, $n = n^{th}$ year after initial investment, r = opportunity cost. (The interest rate used was 5 percent and the depreciation rate 2 percent per year for a total opportunity cost of $r = .07$) and M = maintenance cost (maintenance cost was estimated per gross square foot using a maintenance cost index). The maintenance cost index was provided by the *Building Construction Cost Data*, Robert Snow Means Company Inc., 1979. Where the original cost of the buildings was not available, it was estimated using a construction cost index for gross square footage provided by the Robert Snow Means Company Inc. and the *Building Construction Cost Data* guide for present cost per square foot of various types of structures. This method provided a fairly accurate result when compared with structures for which the cost was known.

7. While the University of Alberta's Office of Institutional Research and Planning presently provides the best data on research, the University has "lost" the data on grants and contracts received by the Faculty of Agriculture prior to 1970. Because these grants and contracts represent a significant and

variable component of expenditures, the data series could not be constructed without its inclusion. The series was compiled for 1970-1980 to test the three universities and six commodities over the last eleven years.

REFERENCES

Agriculture Canada. *Research Branch Report.* Research Branch, Ottawa, various issues.

De Janvry, A. "A Socioeconomic Model of Induced Innovation for Argentine Agricultural Development." *Quarterly Journal of Economics* 87 (August 1973).

Hamilton, D.G. Evaluation of Research and Development in Agriculture and Food in Canada. A report presented to the Canadian Agricultural Research Council, January 1980.

Huffman, Wallace E., and John A. Miranowski. "An Economic Analysis of Expenditures on Agricultural Experiment Station Research." *American Journal of Agricultural Economics* 63, no. 1 (February 1981).

Inventory of Canadian Agricultural Research. A Canadian Agricultural Research Council Report for the Canadian Agricultural Services Coordinating Committee, 1977, 1978-79, 1980.

Peterson, Willis L. "The Allocation of Research, Teaching and Extension Personnel in U.S. Colleges of Agriculture." *American Journal of Agricultural Economics* 51, no. 1 (February 1969).

Report on the Study on the costs of University Research. Canadian Association of University Business Officers, August 1982.

Robert Snow Means Co. *Building Construction Cost Data.* 1979.

Statistics Canada. *Farm Cash Receipts.* Catalogue No. 21-001. Ottawa, Canada, various issues.

_____. *Farm Wages in Canada.* Catalogue No. 21-002. Ottawa, Canada, various issues.

_____. *Farm Net Income.* Catalogue No. 21-202. Ottawa, Canada, various issues.

_____. *Selected Farm Taxfiler Statistics.* Catalogue No. 21-517. Ottawa, Canada, various issues.

_____. *The Consumer Price Index.* Catalogue No. 62-001. Ottawa, Canada, various issues.

_____. *Provincial Government Finance: Revenue and Expenditures.* Catalogue No. 68-207. Ottawa, Canada, various issues.

_____. *Education in Canada: A Statistical Review.* Catalogue No. 81-229. Ottawa, Canada, various issues.

_____. *Census of Agriculture*. Catalogue No. 96-807 to 96-809. Ottawa, Canada, various issues.

Stigler, George. "The Theory of Economic Regulations." *The Citizen and the State*. Chicago, Illinois: Chicago University Press, 1971.

University of Saskatchewan. *Dean of Agriculture Budget*. Faculty of Agriculture (Archives), various years.

_____. *Financial Statements*. Various issues.

_____. *Statistics*. University of Saskatchewan Studies Group, various years.

_____. *Report to the Dean of Agriculture*. Heads of Departments of Faculty of Agriculture (Archives), various years.

_____. *Report to the President*. University of Saskatchewan, various years.

CHAPTER 5

AGRICULTURAL RESEARCH AND INTERNATIONAL TRADE

C. A. Carter

INTRODUCTION

The economic returns to public funds invested in agricultural research in North American have generally been considered to be very high. For exportable U.S. agricultural commodities, such as corn and wheat, the annual internal rates of return have been estimated to be greater than 30 percent (Griliches; Araji, Sim and Gardner; Schultz). Average internal rates of return to research in Canadian grain and oilseeds have been estimated to be at least as substantial as those in the U.S. and, in some cases, even greater (Nagy and Furtan; Zentner). A survey of major studies on the economics of agricultural research has been completed recently by Norton and Davis and thus the literature will not be covered in depth here.

The majority of these studies have employed partial equilibrium domestic models to evaluate the economics of research and have largely overlooked the international trade implications of research and technical change. However, Sarris and Schmitz have suggested that a shift in an exporter's supply function to the right, through research expenditure, could possibly provide large gains to the importer. The major purpose of this paper is to explore the hypothesis raised by Sarris and Schmitz.

In a theoretical context, this paper evaluates the economic effects of agricultural research on a country which exports agricultural commodities and promotes research on them. The objectives are to (a) present a general equilibrium trade model in which the economic effects of research can be assessed, (b) specify the conditions under which the exporting and importing countries gain from research, and (c) identify areas in agriculture where public research funds could maximize benefits to the home country.

The paper extends the partial equilibrium domestic models common in the literature to an agricultural trade model. Conclusions which follow from the model indicate that there is reason to believe that estimates of domestic research benefits from export commodities are highly upward biased. In fact, it is shown that an exporting nation could actually become worse off through research on the export commodity. This result follows from the impact research may have on the exporting country's terms of trade and thus applies only to a "large" country.

A SIMPLE GRAPHICAL MODEL

Assume a Heckscher-Ohlin trade model consisting of two regions: the home country and the foreign country. Each region is endowed with two factors of production — land and capital — and produces two commodities — food and manufactures — under constant returns to scale. Food is land intensive relative to manufactures at all factor prices. Further, assume the home country is a "large" country, which implies the volume of its exports impact on the terms of trade in the international market.

Figure 1 summarizes international equilibrium for the home country. The production possibilities frontier for the home country is shown as M_1F_1 and the

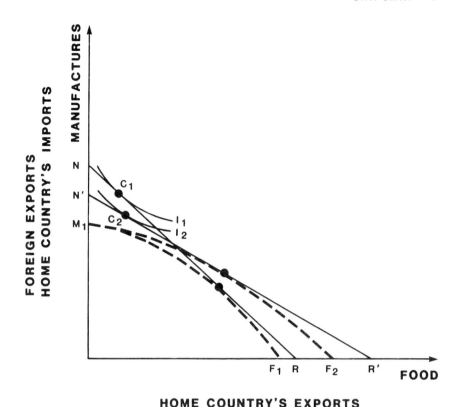

Figure 1

Home Country Equilibrium With Technical Progress in Agriculture

terms of trade line by NR. Assuming the country's tastes are represented by I_1, it initially produces at point P_1 and through trade consumes at point C_1. Thus, the home country exports food and imports manufactures.

Now, consider the effect of agricultural research on the equilibrium production and consumption of the home country. Research and technical progress in the export sector (food) causes the home country's production possibilities frontier M_1F_1 to shift outward to M_1F_2. As a result of food becoming relatively cheaper to produce, the home country's terms of trade may fall from NR to N'R', shifting her production from P_1 to P_2 and the consumption from C_1 to C_2. Since C_2 lies on a lower indifference curve than C_1, it follows that the home country has become worse off.[1]

This model is presented in order to make the point that it may be misleading to equate growth in a nation's capacity to produce more physical output of food, through research and improved technology, with an increase in the nation's welfare. As shown in Figure 1, the deteriorating terms of trade may outweigh the physical effect of technical progress.

The effects of the home country's research and improved technology in food production on the foreign country can be assessed with the aid of Figure 2 where we see that initially the foreign country produces at point P_1 (where her production frontier XY is tangent to the home country's M_1F_1) and consumes at C_1. With technological change in the home country, M_1F_1 shifts to M_1F_2 and the foreign country's production frontier is shifted upward to X'Y' in order to remain tangent to M_1F_2. The foreign country now produces at point P_2 and consumes at C_2. Since C_2 lies on a higher indifference curve than C_1, it is clear that the foreign country has become better off.

The conditions under which the home and foreign country may or may not gain from research are more fully explored in the following section with the aid of a mathematical model.

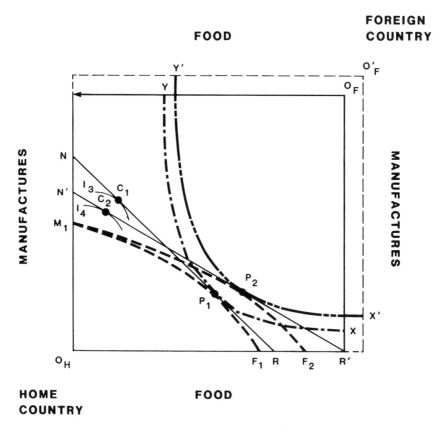

Figure 2

Trade Equilibrium With Technical Progress in Agriculture

A MATHEMATICAL TRADE MODEL

Now, consider a mathematical trade model which assumes that each consumer and producer in both the exporting and importing country is a price taker and that prices adjust instantaneously. Assume we have a two country, two factor world and the home country exports food and imports manufactures. Using duality theory,[2] we can model consumer behaviour by means of an expenditure function and producer behaviour by means of a restricted profit function. The standard assumptions that ensure existence of equilibrium in the model are those of convexity of technology and preferences.

To model production decisions, denote the endowment vector for the primary factors $z = (z_1, z_2) \geq 0$, where z_1 represents the capital endowment and z_2 the land endowment. Let $x = (x_1, x_2)$ be the production vector, with x_1 the output of manufactures and x_2 agricultural food production.

The product price vector is denoted by $p = (p_1, p_2) \geq 0$, with p_1 being the trade price for manufactures and p_2 the trade price for agricultural output. For given trade prices p, and quantities z of primary inputs, the maximized value of output is referred to as the restricted profit function and it can be written as:

$$r(p, Z) = \max_{x} \{ p \cdot x \mid x, Z) \text{ feasible} \} \tag{1}$$

The restricted profit function gives the least upper bound on the level of attainable profits, given p and z, and it has the following properties:

(a) convex in p,

(b) positively linear homogeneous in p for fixed z,

(c) continuous function of p, for $p > 0$, and

(d) concave function of Z for fixed p.

On the consumer side, let $c = (c_1, c_2)$ denote the vector of consumption of manufactures (c_1) and food (c_2), p the vector of their prices, y money income and u the utility function, assumed to be strictly quasi concave. At given prices p, the consumer will attempt to minimize the expenditure necessary to attain a target utility level u. This behaviour can be modelled with the expenditure function, written as:

$$e(p, u) = \min_{c} \{ p \cdot c \mid u(c) \geq u \} \tag{2}$$

The expenditure function has the following properties:

(a) non-decreasing in p,

(b) homogeneous of degree 1 in p,

(c) concave in p, and

(d) continuous in p, for $p > 0$.

Denoting all variables for the home country by lower case letters and those for the foreign country by corresponding upper case letters, international equilibrium is reflected by equations (3) to (6):

$$e\,(p,\,u) = r\,(p,\,Z) \tag{3}$$

$$E\,(P,\,U) = R\,(P,\,Z) \tag{4}$$

$$\frac{\partial e\,(p,\,u)}{\partial p_i} + \frac{\partial E\,(P,\,U)}{\partial P_i} = \frac{\partial r\,(p,\,z)}{\partial p_i} + \frac{\partial R\,(P,\,Z)}{\partial P_i}, \text{ for } i = 1,\,2 \tag{5}$$

$$p = P \tag{6}$$

Equations (3) and (4) express the equality of national income and product in the home and foreign countries, respectively. The market clearing condition for goods 1 and 2 are given by equation (5). The derivatives on the l.h.s. of equation (5) give the Hicksian (compensated) demand functions for manufactures and food in both the home and foreign countries. By the envelope theorem, the r.h.s. of equation (5) gives the optimum output choices (or the supply functions) of manufactures and food. Under the trade, the two countries have the same relative prices for manufactures and food, which is expressed by equation (6). We can also refer to manufactures as the numeraire commodity, which simplifies equation (5).

IMPACT ON THE HOME COUNTRY
OF RESEARCH AND DEVELOPMENT

Now, suppose R&D leads to technological change (such as an improvement in crop yields) in the agricultural industry in the home country. Recall, agricultural production is exported by the home country. We can treat this technological change as an increase in the land base, which is the factor used most intensively in agriculture.[3] Consider the effects of this technological change on trade and utility by introducing a shift parameter Θ in the revenue function of the home country. The general equilibrium conditions are now:

$$e\,(p,\,u) = r\,(p,\,\Theta\,z) \tag{7}$$

$$E\,(P,\,U) = R\,(P,\,Z) \tag{8}$$

$$\frac{\partial e\,(p,\,u)}{\partial p} + \frac{\partial E\,(P,\,U)}{\partial p} = \frac{\partial r\,(p,\,u)}{\partial p} + \frac{\partial R\,(P,U)}{\partial p} \tag{9}$$

$$\frac{p_2}{p_1} = \frac{P_2}{P_1} \tag{10}$$

Differentiating (7) to (10) totally gives us:

$$\frac{\partial e}{\partial u}\,du + \left(\frac{\partial e}{\partial p} - \frac{\partial r}{\partial p}\right)dp = \frac{\partial r}{\partial z}\,dz \tag{11}$$

$$\frac{\partial E}{\partial U} dU + \left(\frac{\partial E}{\partial P} - \frac{\partial R}{\partial P}\right) dP = 0 \tag{12}$$

$$\left(\frac{\partial^2 e}{\partial p^2} + \frac{\partial^2 E}{\partial p^2} - \frac{\partial^2 r}{\partial p^2} - \frac{\partial^2 R}{\partial p^2}\right) dp + \frac{\partial^2 e}{\partial p \partial u} du + \frac{\partial^2 E}{\partial p \partial U} dU = \frac{\partial^2 r}{\partial p \partial z} dz \tag{13}$$

Defining $m = \left(\frac{\partial e}{\partial p} - \frac{\partial r}{\partial p}\right)$ and $M = \left(\frac{\partial E}{\partial p} - \frac{\partial R}{\partial p}\right)$, equations (11) and (12) can be rewritten as:

$$\frac{\partial e}{\partial u} du + m dp = \frac{\partial r}{\partial z} dz \tag{14}$$

$$\frac{\partial E}{\partial U} du + M dp = 0 \tag{15}$$

We can use (14), (15) and (13) to solve for dp, du and dU. Defining the scalar $S = \left(\frac{\partial^2 e}{\partial p^2} + \frac{\partial^2 E}{\partial p^2} - \frac{\partial^2 r}{\partial p^2} - \frac{\partial^2 R}{\partial p^2}\right)$, we can rewrite (13) as:

$$dp = -S^{-1} \frac{\partial^2 e}{\partial p \partial u} du - S^{-1} \frac{\partial^2 E}{\partial p \partial U} dU + S^{-1} \frac{\partial^2 r}{\partial p \partial z} dz \tag{16}$$

Substituting in (14) and (15) and collecting terms, we have in matrix form:

$$\begin{bmatrix} 1 - m{\cdot}S^{-1} \dfrac{\partial c}{\partial y} & - m{\cdot}S^{-1} \dfrac{\partial C}{\partial Y} \\[3mm] m{\cdot}S^{-1} \dfrac{\partial c}{\partial y} & 1 + m{\cdot}S^{-1} \dfrac{\partial C}{\partial Y} \end{bmatrix} \begin{bmatrix} \dfrac{\partial e}{\partial u} du \\[3mm] \dfrac{\partial E}{\partial U} dU \end{bmatrix} = \begin{bmatrix} \dfrac{\partial r}{\partial z} . dz - m{\cdot}S^{-1} \dfrac{\partial^2 r}{\partial p \partial z} dz \\[3mm] m{\cdot}S^{-1} \dfrac{\partial^2 r}{\partial p \partial z} dz \end{bmatrix} \tag{17}$$

Note that in arriving at (17) we know that:

$$\frac{\partial e}{\partial p} = c \text{ and } \frac{\partial^2 e}{\partial p \partial u} = \frac{\partial c}{\partial u} = \frac{\partial c}{\partial y} \quad \frac{\partial y}{\partial u} = \frac{\partial c}{\partial y} \quad \frac{\partial e}{\partial u} \text{ where y denotes}$$

money income.

From (17) we have:

$$\begin{bmatrix} \dfrac{\partial e}{\partial u} du \\[5mm] \dfrac{\partial E}{\partial U} dU \end{bmatrix} = \frac{1}{D} \begin{bmatrix} 1 + m{\cdot}S^{-1} \dfrac{\partial C}{\partial Y} & m{\cdot}S^{-1} \dfrac{\partial C}{\partial Y} \\[3mm] - m{\cdot}S^{-1} \dfrac{\partial c}{\partial y} & 1 - m{\cdot}S^{-1} \dfrac{\partial c}{\partial y} \end{bmatrix} \begin{bmatrix} \dfrac{\partial r}{\partial z} dz - m{\cdot}S^{-1} \dfrac{\partial^2 r}{\partial p \partial z} dz \\[3mm] m{\cdot}S^{-1} \dfrac{\partial^2 r}{\partial p \partial z} dz \end{bmatrix} \tag{18}$$

which simplifies to:

$$
\begin{bmatrix} \dfrac{\partial e}{\partial u} \, du \\[2em] \dfrac{\partial E}{\partial U} \, dU \end{bmatrix} = \frac{1}{D} \begin{bmatrix} \left(1 + m \cdot S^{-1} \dfrac{\partial C}{\partial Y}\right) \dfrac{\partial r}{\partial z} \, dz - m \cdot S^{-1} \dfrac{\partial^2 r}{\partial p \partial z} \, dz \\[2em] \left(- m \cdot S^{-1} \dfrac{\partial c}{\partial y}\right) \dfrac{\partial r}{\partial z} \, dz + m \cdot S^{-1} \dfrac{\partial^2 r}{\partial p \partial z} \, dz \end{bmatrix} \tag{19}
$$

From (19) it follows that the home country gains from technological change if $D > 0$.

$$
(1 + m \cdot S^{-1} \frac{\partial C}{\partial Y}) \frac{\partial r}{\partial z} \, dz - m \cdot S^{-1} \frac{\partial^2 r}{\partial p \partial z} > 0 \tag{20}
$$

To evaluate this expression, note that $\dfrac{\partial r}{\partial z} = \gamma$, is the price of the factor land which is used intensively in the export agricultural good, and $\dfrac{\partial^2 r}{\partial p \partial z} = (\partial \gamma / \partial p)$ is a measure of the effect on the price of the factor with a change in the price of the export good, so in this model $\dfrac{\partial^2 r}{\partial p \partial z}$ is positive for the intensive factor (Stopler-Samuelson theorem). Multiplying (20) through by the scalar S yields:

$$
\left\{ (S + m \frac{\partial C}{\partial Y}) \gamma - m \, (\partial \gamma / \partial p) \right\} dz \leqq 0 \tag{21}
$$

Using this and with some further algebraic manipulation we see that the condition for technological change to be beneficial to the home country becomes:

$$
- \frac{\partial M}{\partial P} (P/M) + \frac{\partial m}{\partial p} (p/m) + p \frac{\partial c}{\partial y} - (\partial \gamma / \partial p) (p/\gamma) > 0 \tag{22}
$$

The first term in expression (22) is the price elasticity of imports of agricultural products for the foreign country; the second is the price elasticity of exports of these products from the home country; the third is the marginal propensity to consume food at home; and the fourth is the Stopler-Samuelson factor price elasticity which measures the proportional change in the price of land associated with a change in the price of agricultural goods.

IMPACT ON THE FOREIGN COUNTRY
OF RESEARCH AND DEVELOPMENT

We have established that technological change in agricultural products may be harmful to the exporting country if the expression in (22) is < 0. It is also of interest to explore the impact of technological change in the home country on the foreign country.

From equation (19) we see that $\dfrac{\partial E}{\partial U}$ is > 0 if and only if:

$$\left(-m{\cdot}S^{-1}\,\frac{\partial c}{\partial y}\right)\,\frac{\partial r}{\partial z}\,dz + m{\cdot}S^{-1}\,\frac{\partial^2 r}{\partial p \partial z}\,dz > 0 \tag{23}$$

We can express (23) as:

$$p\,\frac{\partial c}{\partial y} - \left(\frac{\partial \gamma}{\partial p}\right)\left(\frac{p}{\gamma}\right) < 0 \tag{24}$$

The second term is positive and greater than one while the first term is positive and less than one in a Heckscher-Ohlin world, assuming that food is a normal good and land is used intensively in its production.

Thus we find that what a foreign country gains through technological change, the home country loses.

THE CASE OF NORTH AMERICAN AGRICULTURE

This section aims to discuss the implications of the above results for agricultural research in North America. The discussion is largely centred around expressions (22) and (24) and Figures 3 and 4.

For discussion purposes, consider research conducted in grains and the implications for the U.S. and Canada by evaluating the sign of (22). The first term in this expression represents the price elasticity of imports of grain and it will be positive but extremely low in value because of import trade restrictions which isolate foreign markets from world prices. Tariffs on grain entering the E.E.C. and quotas on Japanese imports provide explicit examples. Recent studies (Abbott; Bredahl, Meyers and Collins; and Zwart and Meilke) strongly suggest that price changes in international grain markets have little effect on import demand or, in other words, the demand functions are highly price inelastic.

The second term in (22) is the price elasticity of exports of grain, which is also positive and probably in the .2 to .4 range (Abbott). The third term is the marginal propensity to consume grain in the home or exporting country and this term will be positive but very low, most likely in the 0.1 to 0.2 range.

Given that the first three terms will be positive but low in value, the sign and magnitude of the fourth term in expression (22) becomes critical. If technological change is treated as an augmentation of land, the intensive factor in grain production, then this fourth term is positive and > 1.0 (the Stopler-Samuelson result).

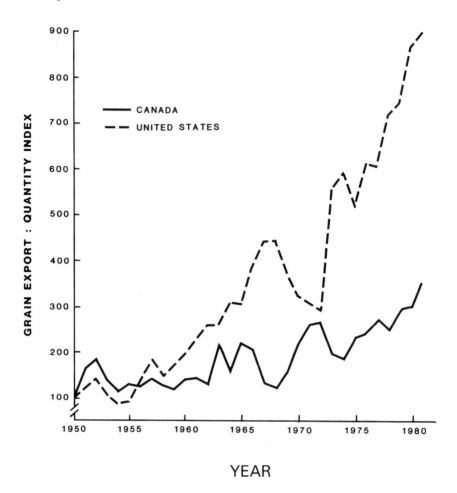

Figure 3

U.S. and Canadian Grain Export Indices: 1950 - 1951

Sources: U.S.D.A. *Agricultural Statistics* (various issues).
          Canadian Wheat Board. *Annual Report* (various issues).

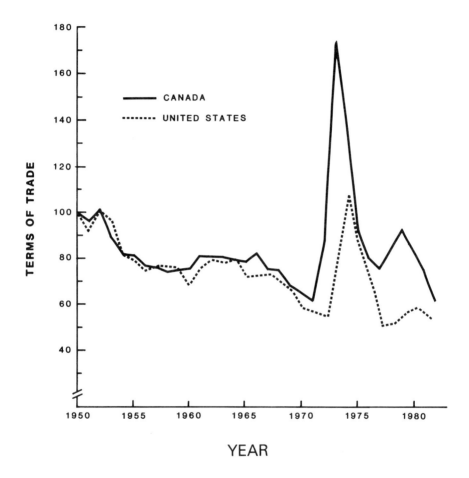

Figure 4

U.S. and Canadian Terms of Trade for Wheat[1]

[1] The terms of trade were calculated as the ratio of an index of annual wheat export prices to a price index for merchandise imports (1950 = 100).

Sources: Statistics Canada. *Canadian Statistical Review* (various issues).
Statistics Canada. *Grain Trade of Canada* (various issues).
U.S. Department of Commerce. *Indexes of U.S. Exports and Imports by Economic Class* (various issues).
U.S.D.A. *Agricultural Statistics* (various issues).

The net result in the case of grain is that the condition in (22) fails to be satisfied and thus technological change harms the home country. As we previously established, this implies that research and development in the home country benefits the foreign country.

This conclusion is supported by the data presented in Figures 3 and 4. Figure 3 clearly shows that export volumes of grain for the U.S. and Canada have grown substantially in the past thirty years. Since the 1950s, the export volume has increased by more than sixfold for the U.S. and has more than doubled for Canada.

The annual terms of trade for U.S. and Canadian agricultural exports, using the price of wheat as a proxy, are shown in Figure 4 for the 1950-1982 period. The terms of trade are calculated by dividing an index of the export price of wheat by an index of the price of imported manufactures. As shown in Figure 4, except for the short-lived 1973-75 commodity boom, the North American agricultural terms of trade have declined by approximately 30-40 percent from the 1950 levels. This deterioration of the terms of trade has largely resulted from increased export volumes of grain and thus serves to offset gains from research and expanded exports.

These observations would, of course, be more robust if we were considering all exporters of wheat as one country as we did in the theoretical model. Australia, Canada and the U.S. account for more than 80 percent of world grain exports and thus we would have to consider only a few countries. Because of similar production practices and technological transferability, it is very difficult to analyze the economic effects of technological change in one country without accounting for the response of its export competitor. If, for example, the U.S. and Canada discontinued wheat-related research and curtailed expansion of export volumes, then Australia could possibly expand its research efforts and impair the North American objectives. Thus, the exporters as a group stand to gain more by jointly recognizing the trade effects of research than does a single country acting on its own.

CONCLUSION

There is no doubt that agricultural research has contributed tremendously to expanded food production in the past. However, this expansion has also made food relatively cheap and thus has altered the food exporters' terms of trade. The message in this paper is that agricultural research in grains may have low rates of return in the exporting nations under the current structure of the grain market.

Employing a standard two country, two factor, two product Heckscher-Ohlin trade model, the conditions under which an exporting country would lose from agricultural research were established. It was suggested that research in grains has not been beneficial to the exporting nations. This result is partially attributable to the protectionist policies of grain-importing nations and their effect on import demand elasticities. Free trade would result in a more elastic import demand function and a terms of trade less sensitive to research and technological change.

This result also implies that agricultural research in North American should be directed toward import-competing products such as fruits and vegetables, dairy products, sugar, and certain grain and oilseed products. The returns to public research spending on import-competing agricultural products would undoubtedly be positive. Alternatively, public research on export goods should be aimed at those commodities which face relatively elastic import demand schedules. This includes primarily oilseeds and processed agricultural products.

NOTES

1. A similar paradox of a growing country becoming worse off with growth was first noted by Edgeworth and then later named "immiserizing growth" by Bhagwati.

2. Duality concepts have been introduced to trade models by Samuelson and Chipman. The model presented here is derived from Dixit and Norman.

3. Jorgensen and Griliches suggest that research and development and technical change can be treated as a special form of input factor accumulation.

REFERENCES

Abbott, P.C. "Modeling International Grain Trade with Government Controlled Markets." *American Journal of Agricultural Economics* 61 (1979): 22-31.

Araji, A.A., R.J. Sim, and R.L. Gardner. "Returns to Agricultural Research and Extension Programs: An Ex Ante Approach." *American Journal of Agricultural Economics* 60 (1978): 964-968.

Bhagwati, J. "Immerserizing Growth: A Geometrical Note." *Review of Economic Studies* 25 (1958): 201-205.

Bredahl, M.E., W.H. Meyers, and K.J. Collins. "The Elasticity of Foreign Demand for U.S. Agricultural Products: The Importance of the Price Transmission Elasticity." *American Journal of Agricultural Economics* 61 (1979): 58-63.

Chipman, J.S. "The Theory of Exploitative Trade and Investment Policies." In *International Economics and Development*, edited by L.E. DiMarco. New York: Academic Press, 1972.

Dixit, A.K., and V. Norman. *Theory of International Trade.* Cambridge: Cambridge University Press, 1980.

Edgeworth, F.Y. "The Theory of International Values." *Economic Journal* 4 (1894): 35-50.

Griliches, Z. "Research Costs and Social Returns: Hybrid Corn and Related Innovations." *Journal of Political Economy* 66 (1958): 419-431.

Jorgensen, D.W., and Z. Griliches. "The Explanation of Productivity Change." *Review of Economic Studies* 34 (1967): 249-283.

Nagy, J.G., and W.H. Furtan. "Economic Costs and Returns from Crop Development Research: The Case of Rapeseed Breeding in Canada." *Canadian Journal of Agricultural Economics* 26 (1978): 1-14.

Norton, G.W., and J.S. Davis. "Evaluating Returns to Agricultural Research: A Review." *American Journal of Agricultural Economics* 63 (1981): 685-699.

Samuelson, P.A. "Prices of Factors and Goods in General Equilibrium." *Review of Economic Studies* 21 (1953): 1-20.

Sarris, A.H., and A. Schmitz. "Towards a U.S. Agricultural Export Policy for the 1980s." *American Journal of Agricultural Economics* 63 (1981): 832-839.

Schultz, T.W. *The Economic Organization of Agriculture.* New York: McGraw-Hill Book Co., 1953.

Zentner, R.P. "An Economic Evaluation of Public Wheat Research Expenditures in Canada." Ph.D. diss., University of Minnesota, 1982.

Zwart, A.C., and K.D. Meilke. "The Influence of Domestic Pricing Policies and Buffer Stocks on Price Stability in the World Wheat Industry." *American Journal of Agricultural Economics* 61 (1979): 434-447.

CHAPTER 6

RATES OF RETURN TO RESEARCH FROM JOINT INVESTMENT: PUBLIC AND PRIVATE

Darrell L. Hueth and Andrew Schmitz

*We thank Ron Cooper and Bob Collender for helpful suggestions and the Lawrence Livermore Lab for financial assistance.

INTRODUCTION

Previous attempts by economists to estimate the rates of return from investment in research and development (R&D) have focused either on social rates of return to public investment or on social and private rates of return to private investment. The ability of the private sector to capture returns from public investment or from joint public and private investment has been largely ignored. One purpose of this paper is to develop a framework for analyzing both social and private returns to public, private and joint investment in R&D.

Also, in previous work there have been no attempts to estimate the ability of input suppliers to benefit from technological change in output production processes. This is important since input suppliers (e.g., chemical companies) contribute money to public institutions for research which affects technological change in the production of the goods requiring use of their inputs. Input suppliers contributing to public research is one example of the main issue which this paper addresses; namely, the rate of return to the private contributor when it is given for research done at public institutions.

Previous estimates of returns to R&D have implicitly assumed perfectly elastic input supply curves. If this assumption does not obtain, ignoring the benefits (losses) accruing to input suppliers can lead to seriously distorted estimated social rates of return to R&D. That is, if the industry in which the R&D expenditures are made affects prices in closely related industries as their output adjusts in response to the R&D, the general equilibrium welfare effects can be quite different from what would be indicated by a partial analysis. Moreover, the partial analysis cannot provide information on the distribution of welfare gains; a question of some importance when evaluating joint public/private investment.

This paper illustrates some of these points with an admittedly simplistic application from the Green Revolution. An estimate of the benefits to the fertilizer industry from the increase in demand caused by the adoption of high-yielding variety (HYV) wheat seeds in India suggests a rate of return considerably in excess of the market rate of interest.

SOME PREVIOUS ESTIMATES OF RATES OF RETURN

As Norton and Davis (1981) point out in their survey of this literature, previous estimates of social and private rates of return can be classified into economic surplus approaches which estimate average rates of return, and regression approaches which can be used to estimate marginal rates of return. The economic surplus approach pioneered by Schultz (1953) calculates R&D induced changes in areas behind supply and demand curves to estimate annual benefits from R&D. This estimate of annual benefits is then divided by total R&D expenditures to provide an estimate of the rate of return on the investment. The most common regression approach regresses the total value of production on conventional inputs and a specified lag structure of R&D expenditures to estimate a marginal value of R&D.

A sampling of empirical results from previous studies is provided in Table 1. Casual perusal of these results supports Evenson, Waggoner and Ruttan's (1979) contention that agricultural research has been a worthwhile social investment. But, the evidence on public investment in other sectors is far less conclusive. In particular, the studies by Terleckyj (1974) and Little (1976) suggest low rates of return to government R&D. Indeed, Kochanowski and Hertzfeld (1981) conclude that the lack of consensus in these studies has generated "the feeling that very little of use to policy makers can be said about the payoffs to government R&D." Perhaps part of the explanation for this "lack of consensus" is simply in the differences of methodologies used to estimate the rate of return.[1] In this paper we focus only on the economic surplus methodology which we believe to be the more general framework of analysis.[2]

TABLE 1

STUDIES OF RATES OF RETURN TO R&D INVESTMENT*

Author	Date	Scope of Research	Estimated Rate of Return/Contribution to Economic Growth			Empirical Methodology
Shultz	1953	Agriculture	Average:	35 to	170%	Computational analysis
Griliches	1958	Hybrid Corn	Internal:	35 to	40%	Cost/benefit
			External:		700%	
Peterson	1967	Poultry	Internal:	20 to	30%	Cost/benefit
Eastman	1967	Military Aircraft:	Marginal: Average:	9 to	40%	Cost/benefit
Weisbrod	1971	Poliomyelitis	Internal:	11 to	12%	Cost/benefit
Ardito & Barletta	1971	Corn, Wheat, etc.	Internal:	54 to	82%	Cost/benefit
Ayer & Schuh	1972	Cotton seed	Internal:		70%	Consumer surplus
Akimo & Hayami	1975	Rice	Internal:	35 to	75%	Consumers and producers surplus
			External:	94 to	554%	
Griliches	1964	Agriculture	Gross:	300 to	1300%	Regression
Mansfield	1965	Manufacturing	Marginal:	2 to	999%	Computational and regression
		Chem & Petrol		30%, 40 to 60%		
Terleckyj	1960	Manufacturing	Not computed			Regression
Kendrick	1961	Selected Indust	Not computed			Regression & computation
Kendrick	1973	Selected Indust	Not computed			Regression & computation
Sahuta	1966	Potash & Sulfur	Not computed			Regression
Minasian	1969	Chemical	Gross:		54%	Regression
Brown & Conrad	1967	Manufacturing	Not computed			Regression
Evanson	1968	Agriculture	Marginal:	46 to	48%	Regression
Solow	1957	Macroeconomic	Tech Progress:		1.5%	Regression

TABLE 1 (Cont'd.)

Author	Date	Scope of Research	Estimated Rate of Return/Contribution to Economic Growth		Empirical Methodology
Denison	1962	Macroeconomic	Tech Progress:	20%	Computational
Denison	1974	Macroeconomic	Tech Progress:	28%	Computational
Jorgenson & Griliches	1967	Macroeconomic	Tech Progress:	2.3%	Computational
Fellner	1970	Macroeconomic	Tech Progress: 13 to	89%	Computational
Midwest Research Institute	1971	Macroeconomic	Over 37%		Regression
Chase Econometrics Assoc.	1976	Macroeconomic	38% to 43%		Regression
Mathematica, Inc.	1975	Specific Innovations	Not computed ($7 billion in benefits for 4 innovations)		Consumers and producers surpluses & subjective
Nestor Terleckyj	1974	2 & 3-digit SIC industry level	Direct: 0% Indirect: 0%		Regression
A.D. Little	1976	Specific Innovations	Not computed (results indicate low rates of return)	Subjective appraisal	

*Source: Adapted from Tables 1 and 2 of Kochanowski and Hertzfeld.

Mansfield, *et al.* (1977) examined the private and social rates of return to private investment in an economic surplus framework. To do this, several cooperating firms were asked to randomly pick one of their recent innovations and provide relevant data. The rates of return were then derived using the following model: Assume the innovator sets the price of his innovation such that he earns t dollars per unit. Furthermore, assume that the firm is competitive and that its supply curve is horizontal as presented in Figure 1. Before the innovation, its supply curve can be represented as S_1 with corresponding price P_1. After the innovation, the supply curve is S_2 and the price is P_2.

The consumer gain is given by area a. The producer's annual increase in economic rents resulting from the innovation is area b and hence the private rates of return to the producer is area b divided by the investment. The social surplus or gain in the market in which the innovation occurs is given by area a + b. Adjustments were then made by Mansfield to account for foregone profits to the innovating and competing firms and for the profits of mimicking firms. The net flow of benefits was then calculated using financial data and information from interviews. From these benefit streams, the internal rates of return were calculated. These are reported in Table 2.

Mansfield's (1977) results are interesting in that the mean private rate of return of about 30 percent is considerably less than the 50 percent rate of return about which agricultural rate of return studies "tend to cluster" (Evenson, *et al.*, 1979).

One is not surprised to find the private rate of return on private investment less than the social rate of return on public or public plus private investment. In point of fact, one is hard pressed to explain a private rate of return approximately an order of magnitude greater than the private lending rate. Adjustment by Mansfield for consumer gains raises the mean rate of return in the private sector to 75 percent. This admittedly small sample of private R&D studies thus suggests at least parity in the private sector with the public sector in terms of social rates of return.

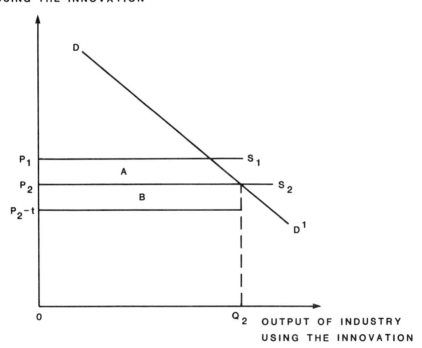

Figure 1

Social and Private Returns from Industrial Innovations

Source: Edwin Mansfield, John Rappoport, Anthony Romeo, Samuel Wagner and George Beardsley, "Social and Private Rates of Return from Industrial Innvoations." *Quarterly Journal of Economics* 91 (May 1977): 221-240.

TABLE 2

SOCIAL AND PRIVATE RATES OF RETURN FROM PRIVATE INVESTMENT IN SEVERAL INNOVATIONS

	Rate of Return (%)	
Innovation	Social	Private
Primary metals innovation	17	18
Machine tool innovation	83	35
Component for control system	29	7
Construction material	96	9
Drilling material	54	16
Drafting innovation	92	47
Paper innovation	82	42
Thread innovation	307	27
Door-control innovation	27	37
New electronic device	Negative	Negative
Chemical product innovation	71	9
Chemical process innovation	32	25
Chemical process innovation	13	4
Major chemical process innovation	56	31
Household cleaning device	209	214
Stain remover	116	4
Dishwashing liquid	45	46
Median	56	25

Source: E. Mansfield, *et al.*

Summarizing, we find that substantial work has been done on estimating social rates of return to public investment and some work has been done on estimating private and social rates of return to private investment. To our knowledge, however, no work has focused on estimating the private rates of return from public contributions to investment in research. In the following section, we develop a methodology which allows us to estimate this return as a special case of a more general joint investment evaluation model.

Before doing so, one can sharpen the focus of our discussion by use of Figure 2. In a typical agricultural industry, public research provides benefits (B) to consumers, producers, processors and input suppliers. Processors and input suppliers can also make contributions (C) to public institutions for research. The general framework used in estimating rates of return to public research (Table 1) lumps public costs and private contributions together and separates out consumers and producer gains showing no effect on processors and input suppliers. On the other hand, Mansfield, *et al.* (Table 2), estimate returns to private research which is done *outside* of public institutions. Our paper focuses on something quite different. We focus on such sectors as processors and input suppliers and their rate of return from their private contribution (C) to what is generally viewed as public research.

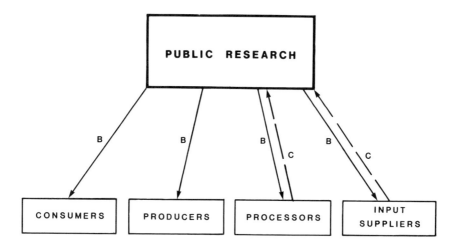

Figure 2

Diagrammatic Representation of Contributions to and Flows of Benefits from Public Research

METHODOLOGY

To analyze private and social rates of return from different types of investment (e.g., public, private and joint) in a specific industry, we define the average social rate of return from investment in a subset of industries all of which purchase all other inputs and sell all other possible outputs except for commodity n under perfect elasticity conditions as

$$r_s = \frac{\Delta C_1 + \sum_{i=1}^{n} \Delta \pi_i}{I_s + \sum_{i=1}^{n} I_{pi}}$$

(1)

where ΔC_1 = change in consumer surplus in industry 1, the only industry in which the R&D investment occurs,

$\Delta \pi_i$ = change in producer surplus or quasi rents in industry i,

I_s = amount of public investment,

I_{pi} = amount of investment from industry i, and

n = number of industries experiencing a change in quasi rents or producer surplus as a result of R&D investment in industry 1.

Similarly, the private rate of return to the ith industry can be defined as

$$r_{pi} = \frac{\Delta \pi_i}{I_{pi}}$$

(2)

and likewise the private rate of return on public investment can be defined as

$$r_{si} = \frac{\Delta \pi_i}{I_s} \tag{3}$$

Consider now a number of special cases:

1. $\Sigma I_{pi} = 0$, $I_s > 0$ or pure public investment

2. $I_s = o$, $I_{pi} > 0$ for some i or pure private investment

3. $I_s > 0$, $\Sigma I_{pi} > 0$, $n > 1$ or joint private/public investment.

The first two cases have been explored extensively in the literature and discussed above. Tables 1 and 2 earlier summarize the results.

Unfortunately, case three has not received much attention in the literature, although some studies in agriculture which have calculated social rates of return to agricultural R&D have assumed private investment to be equal to a constant times the amount of public investment. This may be in part because of the relatively small contribution that the private sector makes to public research. However, there are many cases where, even though the contribution is small, it can shape the direction which research takes.

The analysis of case 3 is a formidable task for a sector consisting of a large number of industries. The identification of consumer and producer gains in each industry requires estimation of a theoretically consistent econometric model of the sector. Fortunately, in agriculture, however, n will be a small number in most applications. Moreover, if one is not concerned about the distributional impact of R&D and appropriate assumptions on the relationships among commodities are met, one may estimate the numerator in equation 1 by simply estimating the general equilibrium supply and demand equations where the innovation occurs, as explained in Just, Hueth and Schmitz (1982, Chapter 9, Appendix D). Again, however, this approach will not allow one to investigate the distributional impacts of joint R&D spending, which we argue is of considerable importance to public and private decision makers.

To better understand this methodology, consider the case of the two industries represented in Figure 3. Industry 1 (Figure 3b) is an input market and industry 2 (Figure 3a) is an output market. Industry 1 is assumed to purchase all inputs under perfectly elastic supply conditions and industry 2 is assumed to purchase all but the output of industry 1 under the same conditions. Input costs rise as output expands in industry 2. The industries are initially in equilibrium at p_1^0, q_1^0 and p_2^0, q_2^0.

Now consider the effect of R&D induced technological change in the output industry 2 which is the result of public research partly funded by input industry 1. As a result of technical change, the partial equilibrium supply curve in Figure 3a shifts from S_2^0 to S_2^1 and in Figure 3b the derived demand curve shifts from D_1^0 to D_1^1. The usual measure of benefits is simply area b + c + f + e in the

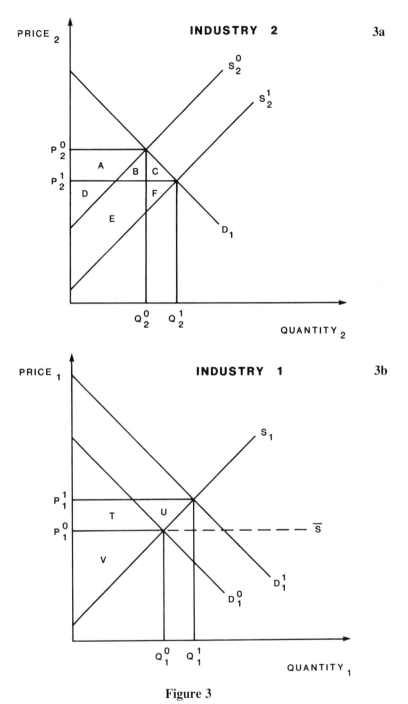

Figure 3

Distribution Effects of Joint Public/Input Industry Investment in an Economic Surplus Framework

output industry 2. This, for example, is the measure suggested by Peterson (1967, p. 571). Note, however, that with the upward sloping supply curve S_1 in Figure 3b there is an increment of quasi rents or producer surplus of area t + u which the Peterson measure fails to capture. Only if the supply curve is $\overline{S}$ in Figure 3b does the Peterson measure provide an appropriate measure of the benefits from R&D.

A large number of possible rates of return on investment can be calculated depending on whether the investment in this industry has been public, private, jointly public and private or jointly private. Our primary interest is the case of joint public/input-industry investment. That is, $I_s > 0$, $I_1 > 0$, $I_2 = 0$. Note that in this case R&D spending by the input industry 1 is for technical change in the output industry 2. This kind of investment can be viewed as demand augmenting technical change from the input suppliers' perspective. In the example in Figure 3 the R&D is supply oriented for the output producer since supply shifts in market 2 from S_2^0 to S_2^1.[3]

This issue of the effects of different types of research is especially intersting in an international trade context. In Figure 4, ES is the excess supply and ED the excess demand before a technological change. The amount exported is q_0 at price p_0. Suppose supply shifts to ES^1 causing D_1^0 in Figure 3b to shift to D_1^1;

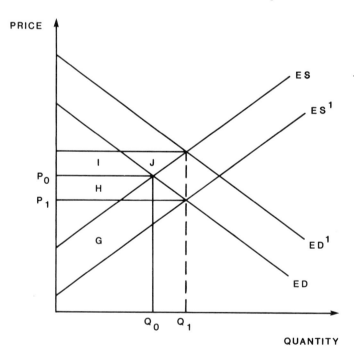

Figure 4

Distribution Effects of Joint Investment in an International Trade Context

the gains to the exporter are area g - area h which may be positive or negative. Now suppose instead the same level of output q is maintained, but a research program which generates a demand shift to ED^1 instead of a supply shift to ES^1 as in Figure 3b. Clearly the gains are now more certain to the export producer since area i + j is clearly positive. In this case the input supplier is indifferent. Thus it may be beneficial to focus joint public and private research on shifting the demand for both the input supplier and for the final product rather than having research which is demand generating for one sector but supply increasing for the other.

The most interesting rates of return that can be calculated from Figure 3 under the above assumptions are:

r_s = area (b + c + e + f + t + u)/(I_s + I_2)
r_{p1} = area (t + u)/I_2
r_{p2} = area (e + f - a)/0

The social rate of return on joint investment r_s provides an unbiased estimate of the rate of return on R&D since it includes the returns to the input industry 1, area t + u. The private rate of return to the output industry 2 from these investments, if positive, will approach infinity since this industry makes no investment. Industry 2 is a free rider. But, it is possible for the output industry 2 to lose as a result of the technical change and hence earn a negative rate of return. In this model, industry 1, the input industry, earns a positive rate of return on its investment I_1. The private rate of return is likely to be greater than what it would have been if it had not been accompanied by public investment. The following section illustrates these input market effects by providing a rough estimate of the benefits to the fertilizer industry from the introduction of high-yielding Mexican wheat in India. Other empirical examples of the private rate of return to investment in public research is also available.

AN ESTIMATE OF THE BENEFITS TO FERTILIZER PRODUCERS FROM ADOPTION OF GREEN REVOLUTION TECHNOLOGY IN INDIAN WHEAT PRODUCTION

The first step in estimating the benefits to the fertilizer industry caused by the adoption of high yielding variety wheat is the estimation of a fertilizer supply curve. Using data from the Food and Agriculture Organization of the United Nations (1972, 1975) the following supply curve was estimated:

P_t = 1461.44 + .467 Q_t R^2 = .829
    (20.07)(6.23)

where
P_t = Price index of one kilo of fertilizer,
Q_t = 1,000,000 tons of fertilizer,

and the figures in parentheses are t ratios.

The next step in obtaining a benefit estimate such as area t + u in Figure 3b is to determine how much fertilizer demand increased with the adoption of HYV. To do this, we used parameter estimates from Maharaja's study of fertilizer demand in Gujarat (Maharaja, 1975). Maharaja found fertilizer use increased 1.12 kilograms per arable hectare for each one-point increase in the percentage of arable land planted to HYVs. This is equivalent to a 1.12 kilogram increase in the quantity demand per hectare of land planted to HYVs. Using the simple formula for the change in producer surplus,

$$\Delta\pi = (p_1 - p_0)(q^0 + \frac{q^1 - q^0}{2})$$

we obtain an estimated increase in benefits to the fertilizer industry of $114 million after the introduction of Mexican wheat in India. In order for this to represent returns to an investment with a 10 percent internal rate of return, the fertilizer industry would have had to invest roughly $85 million in R&D. It seems fair to assume that the rates of return enjoyed by the fertilizer industry from the introduction of HYVs has been far greater than this because the entire budget of the various international plant-breeding stations, to which the private sector directly contributes relatively little, is less than $20 million.

Of course, this is a very simple model which no doubt suffers from simultaneous equation and other biases. Moreover, the price data used in the study were indexed only for Gujarat, not India as a whole. Still, the results are probably a reasonable first order approximation and illustrate the case where input supplies can earn high rates of return from technological change in output industries.

CONCLUDING REMARKS

In this paper we have attempted to show that previous social rate of return on R&D studies have underestimated the rate of return where the industry in which investment takes place has important market relationships with other industries. Welfare effects in these other industries have not usually entered the calculations. Secondly, our analysis of the rate of return models and a rough estimate of the benefits to the fertilizer industry from the introduction of HYV wheat in India suggests that individual or joint private R&D investment in output industries by input-supplying industries can be a rewarding venture from a private standpoint. It was shown that supply side R&D generally increases output but decreases price. Demand-oriented R&D, on the other hand, increases output and price.

Third, this paper has introduced the notion of the private rate of return on public investment generally and on the private contribution to public research. That decision makers are interested in this issue is perhaps best exemplified by the controversy surrounding the issue of U.S. university research on agricultural mechanization which began during the 1970s but still continues. There is a clear need for empirical work on the distribution of the benefits from public R&D expenditures and how the benefits and their distributions are affected by private contributors to public research.

Finally, although not stated, it should be obvious that all of the above work assumed competitive relationships among firms in industries in which technical change occurs. Where non-competitive relationships exist and other distortions are perhaps present, substantial modification of the analysis would be necessary. In this context it is also possible to examine the effect of private, public and joint research on the structure of the producing sector itself. Why did the U.S. poultry industry become so concentrated? Was it because most of the research was done by the private sector so it could capture the rents and thus in the process become more concentrated? One justification for public research is that it should provide benefits to all producers. Public research could be structured to promote competition. Private research may lessen it. In the U.S. grape industry, for example, which is highly concentrated at least in terms of wine making of low- and medium-grape wines, the industry does not seem to be a large supporter of public research in the development of new varieties. Large firms may develop their own varieties for the express purpose of achieving a competitive edge. It appears that the extent to which research is done publicly, privately and jointly could significantly affect the structure of the producing sector.

NOTES

1. Another possible reason for this "lack of consensus" is the non-existence of a delivery system such as the Agricultural Extension Service in other public sectors. Evenson, *et al.* (1979) hypothesized that the institutional characteristics of the land grant system are a large contributor to the estimated high rates of return in the U.S. to agricultural research. KH have speculated that low estimated rates of return to government R&D in the Terleckyj and Little studies may be due to the nature of the innovation resulting from most government R&D. They argue that government (non-agricultural) R&D is usually directed toward new products with inflexible production systems, poorly established marketing demands, no institutional and industrial organization and other characteristics which reduce the immediate economic impact. These speculations are consistent with those of Evenson, *et al.* since agricultural innovations are not likely to have these characteristics.

2. Also, recent econometric results reported at a seminar at the University of California-Berkeley by Professor Oscar Burt cast serious doubt on the validity of the estimates obtained by regression methods.

3. It would be interesting to know the composition of R&D in the agricultural production sector in terms of supply and demand orientations and rates of returns to each. Some industries, such as electric utilities, have a mechanism for pooling R&D funds and investing in almost exclusively marketing-oriented technical change.

REFERENCES

Burt, O. "Some Results on Lag Structures for R&D Expenditures." Seminar presented at University of California, Berkeley, Department of Agricultural and Resource Economics, June 1983.

Evenson, R.E., P.E. Waggoner, and V.W. Ruttan. "Economic Benefits from Research: An Example from Agriculture." *Science* 205 (Sept. 14, 1979): 1101-1107.

Food and Agriculture Organization of the United Nations, 1972, 1975.

Just, R.E., D.L. Hueth, and A. Schmitz. *Applied Welfare Economics and Public Policy*. Englewood Cliffs, N.J.: Prentice-Hall, Inc., 1982.

Kochanowski, P., and H. Hertzfeld. "Often Overlooked Factors in Measuring the Rate of Return to Government R&D Expenditures." *Policy Analysis* 7, no. 2 (1981): 153-167.

Little, A.D., Inc. *Federal Funding of Civilian Research and Development*. Case Studies 2. Washington, D.C., 1976.

Maharaja, M.H. *Demand for Fertilizers: An Analysis of Factors Affecting Demand and Estimation of Future Demand (With Special Reference to Gujarat)*. Baroda, India: Good Companions, 1975.

Mansfield, E., J. Rapoport, A. Romeo, S. Wagner, and G. Beardsley. "Social and Private Rates of Return from Industrial Innovations." *Quarterly Journal of Economics* 91 (May 1977): 221-240.

Norton, G.W., and J.S. Davis. "Evaluating Returns to Agricultural Research: A Review." *American Journal of Agricultural Economics* 63, no. 4 (1981): 685-699.

Peterson, W.L. "Returns to Poultry Research in the United States." *Journal of Farm Economics* 99 (August 1967): 656-669.

Schultz, T.W. *The Economic Organization of Agriculture*. New York: McGraw-Hill Book Co., 1953.

Terleckyj, N. *Effects of R&D on Productivity Growth of Industries: An Exploratory Study*. Washington D.C.: American Enterprise, 1974.

CHAPTER 7

EX ANTE EVALUATION OF A LIVESTOCK BREEDING RESEARCH PROJECT IN CANADA

K. K. Klein

INTRODUCTION

Overall payoffs from investments in agricultural research appear very impressive. Results presented at this Conference, together with studies published elsewhere, show a handsome return to taxpayers for their support of agricultural research activities. These returns have usually been manifested in the form of lower real food prices for consumers, higher quality foodstuffs for the same real price, and higher real returns to owners of primary resources used in the production of agricultural commodities. Results from studies discussed at this Conference may be useful in securing additional funding for agricultural research in Canada, thus increasing the total economic surplus available to members of our society.

A puzzle remains, however. Why is there continual public pressure to reduce or "hold the line" on public expenditures for agricultural research if such substantial payoffs accrue from investing in it? Is the public dissatisfied with the results of agricultural research? Does the public feel that even though they are receiving a generous dividend from this activity, the returns could be even higher? Does the public feel that some of the present research effort is irrelevant?

Twenty-five years ago, an Australian farm management specialist identified three groups of problems he often encountered when using experimental results (Lloyd):

1) lack of economic orientation in experimental design,

2) problems of inference arising from controlled experiments, and

3) considerations of riskiness as applied to use of new techniques.

He urged scientists to design their experiments so that they could yield "more useful information about the profitability of particular practices at different levels, and/or in combination with other practices, under varying sets of economic conditions."

Public pressure to reduce expenditures may merely be a method of forcing reallocation of research effort to try to make the research output more relevant.

Scientific effort can be divided into two purposes: "one is to understand the natural world, the other is to control it" (Tullock, quoting Snow). This motivational dichotomy suggests the distinction between pure and applied research. Cartwright stated that the "sole aim of (pure research was) a fuller *personal* knowledge or understanding of the subject under study." Applied research relates to the felt needs of economic agents "who *directly face* the problems of commerce or society in general."

Funding of agricultural research in Canada is largely earmarked for applied research. Most federal, provincial and industrial research in agriculture has the specified goal of producing information for economic agents "who *directly face* the problems of commerce or society in general."

How should the research director allocate the agricultural research budget, with an eye on trying to obtain the highest possible payoff to society from his or her staff's efforts? Presumably, not all research activities have equal payoffs. Should the research director simply hand the budget to existing scientists and let them allocate the funds? Should more scientists be hired? How about fewer scientists and more technicians? Is the design of experiments adequate? Lloyd suggested that designs for many agricultural experiments led to problems in use of research results. Are there any economic principles that could be used to guide these budget allocation decisions so that more relevant research and, hopefully, a higher payoff to society would result?

The overall objective of this study was to determine whether economic criteria could be successfully employed to obtain greater productivity in the research process itself. Research productivity can be defined as the value of information produced per dollar of research expenditure.

This study involved a number of steps. First, an economic framework had to be assembled to permit an evaluation of various types of data collected in an agricultural research project. Second, results from a partially completed research project on foreign cattle breeds in Canada were analyzed within the economic framework to project the expected competitiveness of various breed crosses. Finally, actual results from the completed research project were examined to see whether use of the economic framework would have permitted a more efficient allocation of research resources.

ECONOMIC FRAMEWORK

A decision maker is central to all problems of choice. He or she must choose among alternative courses of action. The purpose of an applied research project is to provide the decision maker with information regarding the outcomes of alternative courses of action. Research information that is valuable would permit lower per unit production costs for the same quality of output or higher quality products (as perceived by consumers) for the same level of input costs.

Who is the relevant decision maker when considering agricultural research? Is it the public funding agency that allocates its resources among the disparate concerns of national defense, highway construction, consumer information and agricultural research? Is it the research leader who coordinates resources utilized in several related research projects? Is it the scientist who must select the experimental design for testing specific hypotheses? Or, more fundamentally, is it the farmer producer who will or will not change his production techniques as a result of the information from the research projects?

The purpose of conducting applied agricultural production research must be to provide information for the farmer producer. He is the decision maker who must weigh the evidence produced by the research projects and make a judgement about its value to his own production activities. He is the decision maker who must make adjustments to his farming operations to apply the results of research projects. He is the decision maker who, by his choice of actions, ultimately determines whether society will gain from engaging in specific types of agricultural research activities.

Researchers and research administrators must decide upon research strategies to be followed for producing the required information. Since alternative research strategies can be more or less costly, and since they can produce more or less valuable information for the entrepreneur, some criteria must be used to choose among them. Economic evaluations conducted at the farm level, i.e., where decisions are made regarding commodities to produce and methods of production, may be helpful in making these decisions.

The entrepreneur attempts to maximize his utility (in this study, minimize total costs for a given level of output) by choosing among the available production alternatives. The selected production alternatives, combined with an unknown state of nature and the manager's own personal characteristics, produce some output. Market-determined prices of inputs and outputs act as the choice indicators for the entrepreneur's decisions.

The entrepreneur's ability to select among the available production alternatives is conditioned by how well he understands the consequences of each. In other words, the amount and type of information available to him directly affects his decision-making ability and indirectly influences the level of utility he is able to achieve.

Complete information for the entrepreneur requires a complete specification of the dimensions and elements of the production opportunity set (Figure 1). Specifically, this includes:

1) the feasible production alternatives $(a_i, i = 1...m)$ available to him,

2) the states of nature $(s_j, j = 1...n)$ that may occur, and the probability of each state of nature occurring, and

3) the outcomes (u_{ij}) of all production alternatives under all states of nature, given the nature of his managerial input.

PRODUCTION ALTERNATIVES	STATES OF NATURE					
	s_1	s_2	s_3	s_4	...	s_n
a_1	u_{11}	u_{12}	u_{13}	u_{14}	...	u_{1n}
a_2	u_{21}	u_{22}	u_{23}	u_{24}	...	u_{2n}
a_3	u_{31}	u_{32}	u_{33}	u_{34}	...	u_{3n}
a_4	u_{41}	u_{42}	u_{43}	u_{44}	...	u_{4n}
.		.				
.		.				
.		.				
a_m	u_{m1}	u_{m2}	u_{m3}	u_{m4}	...	u_{mn}

Figure 1

Manager's Production Opportunity Set

Of course, this informational requirement could never be completely satisfied, due to the vastness of the production opportunity set and the unquantifiable nature of some of its elements. Moreover, there would be a cost attached to determining this information. It would be irrational to seek and acquire data past the point where the extra gain attached to its recovery exceeded the extra cost of its procurement.

The concept of an Innovation Possibility Frontier (IPF) has been employed to help understand the direction of technical change. The IPF bounds the current state of knowledge that is relevant to the production of a given commodity. Ahmad described the IPF as "an envelope of all the alternative isoquants (representing a given output on various production functions) which the business-man expects to develop with the use of the available amount of innovating skill and time...." It is not necessary that every possible isoquant be technically feasible at the time of the analysis. It is only necessary that they *could* be developed given the current state of knowledge and skills.

Ahmad developed a 2-factor model that demonstrated the Hicksian notion of induced technical change, i.e., production of the same output using fewer resources (Figure 2). During the current time period, one unit isoquant (UI_C) has been developed and is utilized by entrepreneurs. Other unit isoquants could have been developed along the IPF but UI_C is the one with the lowest total cost when the price ratio is P_1P_2.

Substitution of factors along UI_C would occur if the factor price ratio changed during the current time period. A permanent shift in the factor price ratio to P_5P_6 would lead in the short term to substitution of factor 2 for factor 1; however, the currently used isoquant (UI_C) would no longer be optimal. Another unit isoquant (UI_A) could be developed within the IPF that would enable the production of the same output at a lower total cost (P_3P_4 is parallel to P_5P_6), assuming constant returns to scale. The IPF concept can be used in a normative as well as a descriptive sense. Different unit isoquants can be simulated on the basis of experimental data and notions or images of the future. Researchers and research administrators must decide which of the alternative unit isoquants to investigate and develop.

Simulation of a unit isoquant requires identification and separation of produc-tion methods into sets that represent a single technology and are fundamentally different from each other. For example, different breed crosses of beef cattle can be considered as different technologies. A unit isoquant can be simulated for each breed cross. Output represented by each unit isoquant (e.g., cwt of weaned calves) can usually be obtained with various ratios of inputs. Some may be more capital intensive; others may be more labour intensive. Input requirements for each production alternative within each unit isoquant must be computed.

The envelope of all unit isoquants is the IPF. If a unit isoquant lies above the IPF in all input dimensions it can be said that the particular technology represented by that isoquant is dominated. It is technologically inefficient and it can never be economically efficient.

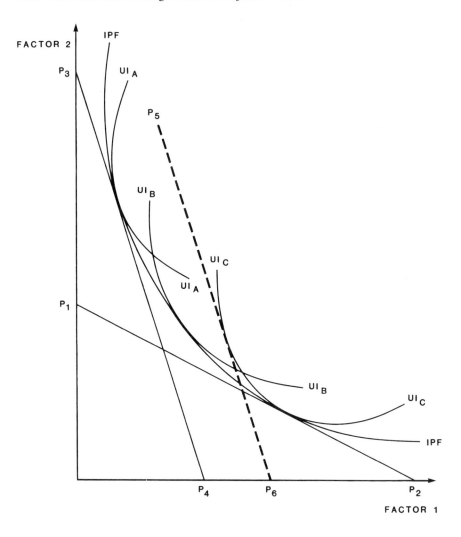

Figure 2
Ahmad's Induced Innovation Model

PRIOR ANALYSIS OF FOREIGN CATTLE BREED PROJECT

A large beef breeding research project conducted by Agriculture Canada was evaluated in the economic framework described above. The Foreign Cattle Breed Evaluation (FCBE) project was initiated in 1968. Its purpose was to determine the reproductive performance of crossbred cattle by mating Hereford, Shorthorn and Angus cows with bulls from the newly introduced breeds of Charolais, Simmental and Limousin. A tenth group, "the commercially popular Hereford X

Angus cross'' was used as the experimental control. The reproductive performance of these hybrid females was to be evaluated over a period of five calf crops in western Canada.

The ten groups of females were allocated randomly to two contrasting environments: Brandon, Manitoba (black soil zone, moderate rainfall, intensive grazing) and Manyberries, Alberta (brown soil zone, low rainfall, extensive grazing). Approximately 500 cows were allocated to each location. The management and nutrition at each location were "designed to conform with traditional commercial practices in that region."

The hybrid heifers were bred as yearlings to one of a sample of Red Angus and Beefmaster bulls. Subsequent breedings were to one of a sample of Charolais, Simmental, Limousin and Chianina bulls. All matings were three-way crosses, i.e., no backcrossing was done. This resulted in thirty-one breed crosses at each of the two locations for the second phase of the project (nine hybrid females X three bull breeds plus the control Hereford-Angus cows X four bull breeds).

The FCBE project was designed to yield data on breeding and gestation characteristics, calving weights and difficulties, weaning weights and ages, feed-lot consumption and growth, and carcass characteristics.

A systems model of a beef-forage-grain farm in western Canada (Klein and Sonntag) was adapted to simulate unit isoquants for each of the ten breed crosses of females using production data from only their first calves. Feed requirements of the various breed crosses were estimated from the cow's weight and rate of gain. Measurement of actual feed consumption by the various breed crosses will be done in a future phase of the FCBE project. A variety of production methods that involved various ratios of labour to capital was simulated. Labour and capital were each disaggregated into several categories to permit an analysis of intra-year variation in opportunity costs for each resource.

Production levels for each of the ten groups of cattle were estimated, based on data from only first calf production. An IPF was constructed to envelope the ten unit isoquants, one for each breed. Cost disadvantages for the non-optimal breed crosses were estimated under a wide range of input price ratios.

Results from this investigation of first calf performance were reported in Klein and Kehrberg. In general, two breed crosses (enumerated as breeds 1 and 6 in the earlier study) had lower per unit costs than the others under the wide array of economic scenarios tested. Four breed crosses (breeds 4, 5, 7 and 10) had small cost disadvantages under certain factor price relatives. The other four breed crosses (breeds 2, 3, 8 and 9) appeared to be genuinely non-competitive, given data from these breeds as displayed in their first calf performance.

It was considered that some of the early observations on these seemingly non-competitive breed crosses could have unrealistically biased the results to show them to be less competitive than they really were. Since no estimates were available at the time on variations in recorded data, the value of three important performance characteristics (average daily gain for calves, birth weight of calves, and calving rate for cows and replacements) were increased for one breed cross (breed 2) to values that were equal to those of the highest recorded for all breeds in the project. Each alteration to the data was analyzed separately. A new IPF was generated where breed 2 had these advantages in biological performance over its actual recorded data.

Results of this further analysis confirmed the non-competitiveness of this second breed, even under the very optimistic assumptions regarding several of the performance characteristics. The results indicated a lack of sensitivity of this breed to any changes in relative prices of resources. This breed appeared to be dominated by the other breed crosses and thus could be regarded as technologically inefficient.

It was suggested that a more efficient use of research resources could be obtained if some of these seemingly non-competitive breed crosses could be eliminated from the research project and resources shifted elsewhere. However, no changes were made to the design of the research project. It continued on to completion of the second phase, i.e., the three-way crosses with each of the ten groups of hybrid cows at two locations. Performance data were collected from five calf crops for each of the thirty-one breed crosses.

POSTERIOR ANALYSIS OF FOREIGN CATTLE BREED PROJECT

Biological results have been published from the second phase of the FCBE project (Fredeen, et al., 1977; Fredeen, et al., 1979; Fredeen, et al., 1982a; Fredeen, et al., 1982b; Lawson, 1983). An economic analysis was conducted on all thirty-one breed crosses from this phase of the research project. This permitted a comparison with the evaluation of first calf data to determine the overall usefulness of the economic framework in increasing efficiency of resource use in agricultural research.

Representative farms from each of the two soil zones included in the FCBE project were simulated over a wide array of economic conditions to gauge relative performance of each of the thirty-one breed crosses.

What did the economic analysis of the second phase of this research project tell us about the usefulness of this economic framework in guiding the design and conduct of the beef-breeding project? Could research resources have been saved or reallocated without diminishing the value of information from this project?

The four breed crosses that appeared non-competitive (breeds 2, 3, 8 and 9) when analyzed on only first calf data were generally very non-competitive when crossed with bulls of any of the other three "exotic" breeds. Differences in net farm income ($/cow) and relative rank of each of the four seemingly non-competitive breeds are presented in Table 1.

None of the breed combinations from the four groups of hybrid females was optimal in either of the two locations. Generally, breed crosses from these four

TABLE 1

**DISADVANTAGE IN NET INCOME PER COW
FROM OPTIMAL BREED, TWO LOCATIONS**

COW	SIRE BREED[1]							
BREED[2]	Char.	Sim.	Lim.	Chian.	Char.	Sim.	Lim.	Chian.
	BLACK SOIL ZONE				BROWN SOIL ZONE			
2	NA	$78	$37	$70	NA	$27	$2	$42
		(28)[3]	(14)	(25)		(9)	(2)	(18)
3	NA	$42	$32	$23	NA	$28	$30	$26
		(16)	(11)	(7)	(10)	(11)	(8)	
8	$91	$47	NA	$21	$108	$41	NA	$33
	(30)	(20)		(3)	(31)	(17)		(12)
9	$43	$44	NA	$58	$10	$16	NA	$53
	(17)	(18)		(24)	(30)	(5)	(23)	

[1] Abbreviated sire breeds refer to Charolais, Simmental, Limousin and Chianina, respectively.

[2] Cow breed indicates a coded breed cross as reported in Klein and Kehrberg.

[3] Net farm income rank out of 31 breed crosses in each location.

groups of hybrid females were ranked in the bottom half of the thirty-one breed crosses. However, two combinations in the brown soil zone and one in the black soil zone did rank in the top five at these locations. Realistically, only one combination (Limousin terminal sire bred to the second breed in the brown zone) appeared to be competitive. It was the only combination among the four groups of hybrid females that had a net income disadvantage from the optimal breed cross of less than $16/cow.

The results of this study are somewhat unclear. If the four groups of hybrid females had been dropped from the research project, one potentially competitive breed combination in one location would have been lost. On the other hand, as much as 40 percent of the very considerable research resources used in this project could have been redeployed. They could have been used to examine the relative competitiveness of other non-tested large breeds, to gather data on input requirements of the six remaining groups of hybrid cows (which was deferred to a future phase), or used on some other agricultural research project that promised large rewards.

Still, finding the one relatively competitive breed combination is disturbing. It is troubling to realize that it could have been missed if the proposed economic framework was used as an objective guide for selection of treatments in the research project. On reflection, though, a number of factors may have intervened on the dismissal of this or other treatments had the economic framework been employed. The first calf performance on which the IPF was generated contained data on only about two-thirds of the first calves. Data were not disaggregated by location at that time. Bulls used on the first calf heifers were from relatively small breeds (Red Angus and Beefmaster) to reduce calving difficulties. Results from the large breed bulls could be expected to show a different pattern of results.

In all likelihood, the use of an economic framework such as the one proposed in this study would be employed in a screening capacity where the ten most competitive groups of hybrid females could have been selected from a somewhat larger number of contestants. The procedure could also be used in combination with periodic reviews of the research project. Whenever a point has been reached where no valuable information can be forthcoming from some part of an agricultural research project, efficiency of resource use demands that no further resources are spent on it.

DISCUSSION

The major objective of applied agricultural research must be to produce information that would permit lower per unit production costs (or higher quality products in the perception of consumers, with the same costs of production). The specific objectives of most applied research projects can be outlined in a manner which permits quantitative economic analyses. The degree of precision required in estimates of the parameters under investigation can be analyzed prior to commencement of the project. The value of this information depends upon the prior level of knowledge and the increase in economic efficiency possible with more precise knowledge.

The expected value of more precise information can also be used to guide the experimental design and choice of model in the contemplated research project.

Project reviews can occur at various stages between initiation and completion of a research project. They provide opportunities to reassess the objectives of the project, to determine the information already gained, and to plan future courses of action in a related area.

If opportunities are available for project redesign or termination at the project review stage, an economic evaluation of the incomplete data can be especially helpful. This can be accomplished by interacting formal evaluation procedures with research personnel who have prior expectations. Thus, analyses can be performed to determine the progress of information gathering activities. If the information objectives of the experiment are met prematurely, the value of additional resources committed to the project is zero. Similarly, if it can be determined that suitable progress is not being made in obtaining the required information, alternative experimental procedures can be considered.

Following the completion of a research project, an economic evaluation can be undertaken to determine the degree to which the project's objectives were met. This evaluation can be used to guide further research efforts. The areas where more precise estimates of selected parameters would provide valuable information can be identified.

Evaluation of research projects can take the form of a series of investigations throughout the life of the research projects. As each project develops from early conceptualization, project planning and initiation, through to completion, the degree to which (expected) research results satisfy the economic criteria will likely change. Formal evaluation procedures such as the one used in this study can be employed to monitor and guide their progress.

REFERENCES

Ahmad, Syed. "On the Theory of Induced Invention." *Economic Journal* (June 1966): 344-357.

Cartwright, Richard Wayne. "Research Management in a Department of Agricultural Economics." Ph.D. diss., Purdue University, West Lafayette, Indiana, 1971.

Fredeen, H.T., J.E. Lawson, J.A. Newman, and G.W. Rahnefeld. "Reproductive Performance of Foreign X Domestic Hybrid Cows Under Two Management Systems." Ottawa, Canada: Agriculture Canada Publication 1632, 1977.

Fredeen, H.T., J.A. Newman, J.E. Lawson, and G.W. Rahnefeld. "Preweaning and Postweaning Performance of Progeny Sired by Charolais, Simmental, Limousin, and Chianina Bulls Mated With Exotic First-Cross Dams." Ottawa, Canada: Agriculture Canada Publication 1682, 1979.

Fredeen, H.T., G.M. Weiss, J.E. Lawson, J.A. Newman, and G.W. Rahnefeld. "Environmental and Genetic Effects on Preweaning Performance of Calves From First-Cross Cows. I. Calving Ease and Preweaning Mortality." *Canadian Journal of Animal Science* 62 (March 1982): 35-49.

Fredeen, H.T., G.M. Weiss, G.W. Rahnefeld, J.E. Lawson, and J.A. Newman. "Environmental and Genetic Effects of Preweaning Performance of Calves From First-Cross Cows. II. Growth Traits." *Canadian Journal of Animal Science* 62 (March 1982): 51-67.

Klein, K.K., and E.W. Kehrberg. "The Use of an Innovation Possibility Frontier to Evaluate an Applied Animal Breeding Research Project." *Canadian Journal of Agricultural Economics* 29 (July 1981): 141-158.

Klein, Kurt K., and Bernard H. Sonntag. "Bioeconomic Firm Level Model of Beef, Forage, and Grain Farms in Western Canada: Structure and Operation." *Agricultural Systems* 8 (1982): 41-53.

Lawson, John E. "Evaluation of Exotic Crosses of Beef Cattle Under Extensive Range and Semi-Intensive Cultivated Pasture Conditions." Presented to District Agriculturists meeting, Lethbridge, Alberta, May 1983. (Mimeographed.)

Lloyd, Alan G. "Agricultural Experiments and Their Economic Significance." *Review of Marketing and Agricultural Economics* 26 (1958): 185-209.

Tullock, Gordon. *The Organization of Inquiry*. Durham, North Carolina: Duke University Press, 1966.

EMPIRICAL STUDIES ON
ECONOMICS AND
AGRICULTURAL RESEARCH

CHAPTER 8

RETURNS TO A PROVINCIAL ECONOMY FROM INVESTMENTS IN AGRICULTURAL RESEARCH: THE CASE OF ONTARIO

George L. Brinkman and Barry E. Prentice

INTRODUCTION

Ontario has made significant improvements in agricultural production over the past several decades. Only twenty-five years ago, Ontario had to import significant volumes of feed in order to maintain a level of livestock production that was only half its current (1983) output, the work-force employed in agriculture was twice as large, and over a million additional acres of land were cropped. These improvements in labour and land productivity have resulted directly from a sustained growth in investment in agricultural research, extension and education.

This paper provides an assessment of the benefits to investments in Ontario agriculture through research and supporting services. The overall conceptual framework is discussed first, followed by a more detailed analysis of the calculations for measuring research and supporting services investments, benefits from research and rates of returns. The study next provides a sensitivity analysis of the various assumptions and calculations, and concludes with a discussion of implications of research funding for future agricultural benefits.[1]

PROCEDURE FOR MEASURING RETURNS TO ONTARIO AGRICULTURAL RESEARCH

In this study the aggregate returns from agricultural research and supporting services were measured as the benefits from inputs saved in Ontario food production as a result of research improvements relative to the costs of investments in research and supporting services. Investment costs, consisting of provincial, federal and private agricultural research, production-oriented extension and agricultural education, were analyzed for a twenty-three year period from 1950-1972. Benefits, in turn, were lagged behind expenditures by six years to account for the length of time to put new research discoveries into place and were measured over the 1956 to 1978 period. Total inputs saved by agricultural research innovations were measured as the inputs that would have been required in the absence of research using 1951-55 average technology (yields; feeding rations; capital, land and labour per unit of output; etc.) to generate the actual food production in Ontario each year *minus* the actual quantity of inputs used. In addition, the 1978 level of benefits was extended for twenty years at a 5 percent straight-line depreciation rate per year to account for continuing benefits from the 1950 to 1972 research expenditures that would be available for several years into the future beyond 1978, but would decline in value as they became obsolete or superceded by new discoveries.

GENERAL ASSUMPTIONS, ADJUSTMENTS AND BIASES

In this study a number of assumptions had to be made on such factors as the source and distribution of benefits, multiplier effects, relative prices and quality of inputs and outputs. Some of these assumptions likely overestimate the overall value of research while others underestimate it. On balance, however, it appears likely that the overall assumptions and measurement methods used in this study provide a net underestimation of the total benefits, rather than an overestimation.

Source of Benefits

One of the most important assumptions employed in the study which tends to overestimate the value of research is that agricultural research and supporting services are identified as the sole sources of the savings in inputs. In contrast, it can be argued that other factors could have easily contributed to savings in inputs, such as the improvement in average productivity brought about by the withdrawal/consolidation of less productive farm units, the improvement in the quality of inputs such as the managerial competence of farmers, and the migration from agriculture that might have occurred alone in response to rising relative non-farm wage rates.

To avoid most of these limitations, several adjustments were made in the methodology and data. First, investments complementary to agricultural research in specialized agricultural education and extension were included as supporting services with agricultural research to help account for factors contributing to the ability of farmers to improve their farm management skills and their ability to consolidate larger farm units. In addition, these supporting services have had an important role in facilitating the adoption of labour-saving technology and changes in farm structure, leading to increased migration to non-farm jobs. Second, farm labour inputs were adjusted to reflect the improvement in the quality of farm labour that has occurred because of increased levels of general education (other than agricultural education), which in turn should help to account for potential off-farm migration induced from outside agriculture. Third, all agricultural research expenditures by the private sector in Ontario were included, except for market research and advertising which were assumed to be inappropriate for affecting production technology or included in the price of farm inputs. Finally, all data were carefully reviewed and culled of subsidies, cultural supports and other non-production-oriented expenditures.

Benefit Spillovers

Benefit spillovers occur when research in one area provides benefits that become available free of charge by "spilling over" into another area. Benefits spilling into an area typically overestimate the value of research because the full cost of technological change is not measured, while benefits spilling out of an area underestimate research returns. Unfortunately, benefit spillovers can be very difficult to identify and measure precisely.

In this study it was assumed that benefits from research and supporting services spilling over into Ontario were approximately equal to benefits spilling out of Ontario and therefore would cancel each other out. This assumption has the potential of overestimating the value of Ontario agricultural research because of the large potential for benefit spillins occurring from research conducted in the United States and other parts of Canada. Spillovers from Ontario to the United States are likely to be fewer in number than those into Ontario. On the other hand, spillouts from Ontario may be of equal value to spillins given the much larger size of U.S. agriculture.[2] As a consequence, equality between research benefit spillins and spillouts seems a reasonable assumption. Furthermore, any overestimation of research benefits from research spillins is likely offset by an underestimation from educational spillouts due to a net outflow of Canadian and foreign students trained in Ontario working in other areas.

Second Round Effects

In addition to direct benefits, agricultural research also may generate substantial indirect benefits through the impact of increased agricultural production on processing, distributing and retailing industries. At times, the benefits from increased employment and income in these sectors may even exceed the direct benefits in agricultural production. In this study, however, indirect multiplier effects have been ignored, substantially underestimating the overall impact of agricultural research and supporting services. Furthermore, no account has been taken for changes in output quality, such as better quality meats, and food price impacts generated by agricultural research. In the absence of research, Canada would not have been able to produce its domestic requirements of food, leading to higher food prices, loss of food sector employment to other countries, higher wage demands and reduced competitiveness throughout the entire economy. These benefits also could be very significant.

Other effects which were not examined included general equilibrium effects and questions of equity (i.e., income distribution), migration and market concentration. Negative secondary effects of agricultural research, such as environmental damage, also were ignored.

INVESTMENTS IN ONTARIO AGRICULTURAL RESEARCH AND SUPPORTING SERVICES

The components of investment expenditures in agricultural research and supporting services consist of operating and capital expenditure allocations for:

1) Ontario Government agricultural research,

2) Ontario Government agricultural education,

3) Ontario Government production-oriented extension,

4) Federal Government agricultural research attributable to Ontario, and

5) Private agricultural research attributable to Ontario.

Agricultural education and production-oriented extension expenditures were included as part of the overall investment in technological change because they are complementary and mutually supportive to research in improving agricultural productivity. Many good research discoveries might remain unused, or if adopted would not be utilized as quickly, without education and extension services to teach farmers how to use the new technology. Agricultural education and extension represent about 30 percent of the total investment costs.

TABLE 1

ANNUAL AGGREGATE NET REAL INVESTMENTS IN
AGRICULTURAL RESEARCH AND SUPPORTING SERVICES
BY THE ONTARIO GOVERNMENT, THE ALLOCATION TO ONTARIO OF
AGRICULTURAL RESEARCH EXPENDITURES
BY THE FEDERAL GOVERNMENT AND THE AGRICULTURAL RESEARCH
EXPENDITURES MADE IN ONTARIO BY THE PRIVATE SECTOR,
1950/51-1972/73

Year	Ontario Government Research and Education[a]	Ontario Government Extension	Federal Government Research	Private Sector Research	Annual Aggregate Net Real Investment in Agricultural Research and Supporting Services[b]
	(thousands of dollars expressed in constant 1978 values)[c]				
1950/51	$ 10,720	$ 7,061	$ 8,633	$ 2,494	$ 28,909
51/52	11,037	6,905	7,271	3,619	28,833
52/53	12,621	7,246	7,814	4,845	32,526
53/54	13,299	7,607	8,336	6,369	35,611
54/55	14,789	7,950	9,939	7,928	40,606
55/56	15,277	8,584	9,342	8,825	42,028
56/57	17,849	9,585	9,672	10,516	47,622
57/58	26,954	11,196	12,870	11,477	62,497
58/59	27,177	11,597	11,345	13,159	63,278
59/60	26,266	11,442	11,318	13,772	62,798
1960/61	25,714	11,500	9,355	15,060	61,629
61/62	23,109	12,147	12,439	15,000	62,695
62/63	24,059	12,203	9,890	18,434	64,586
63/64	29,996	13,234	10,272	18,052	71,554
64/65	30,696	13,842	10,467	21,179	76,184
65/66	29,684	14,507	14,536	20,574	79,301
66/67	29,785	15,729	15,309	21,215	82,038
67/68	33,737	17,777	17,994	23,600	93,108
68/69	35,877	15,016	24,401	22,495	97,789
69/70	41,095	16,146	18,551	23,746	99,538
1970/71	42,866	17,272	21,896	23,411	105,445
71/72	46,902	18,538	21,865	22,716	110,021
72/73	43,270	18,596	21,587	22,073	105,526
Total[b]	$612,780	$285,681	$305,102	$350,559	$1,554,122

[a] Research and education expenditures included together as some research and education expenses reported jointly in the public accounts.

[b] Subject to error because of rounding.

[c] Deflated by the Consumer Price Index

Source: Ontario expenditures from *Ontario Public Accounts*, Federal Government expenditures from *Public Accounts of Canada* and private research expenditures from mail survey.

Data for public expenditures were taken from public accounts. Federal research expenditures for experimental stations located in Ontario were allocated 100 percent to Ontario while those located outside the province were excluded. Expenditures for national research branches and institutes (primarily located in Ottawa and serving the entire country) were allocated to Ontario on the basis of Ontario's share of gross revenue in order to reflect the benefits that would accrue on the basis of total production. Private research expenditures were obtained by survey of private companies across Canada, with expenditures included for Ontario if they occurred in the province. Privately-funded agricultural extension and education expenditures (advertising and company representatives) were excluded because they were assumed to be included in the prices charged for farm inputs. Research expenditures in non-agricultural research areas also were ignored.

Data on investment costs for agricultural research and supporting services are presented in Table 1 in 1978 constant dollars for 1950/51 through 1972/73. Overall total real investment increased from about $29 million in 1950/51 to about $106 million in 1972/73.

BENEFITS OF AGRICULTURAL RESEARCH

The benefits of agricultural research were calculated through a complex procedure summarized in notation form in Appendix A. In general terms, the actual inputs used in Ontario agriculture and the output they generated were first measured over the 1951 to 1978 period. To calculate the extra inputs that would have been required without research, an Input Requirement Generator Model (IRGM) was constructed to simulate the historical input-output relationships of each commodity for the 1951-55 base period. The IRGM was used to calculate the hypothetical required inputs that would have been needed to produce the actual output of each commodity each year from 1956 to 1978 by using the fixed technology of the 1951-55 base period. The benefits, measured by the inputs saved, were determined by subtracting the actual inputs used from the hypothetical required inputs produced by the IRGM.

INPUT REQUIREMENT GENERATOR MODEL

A schematic diagram of the IRGM is presented in Figure 1. The IRGM reverses the normal flow of inputs and outputs in the agricultural system by first starting with given quantities of outputs and then calculating the inputs required to produce these outputs. Overall, seventeen crops and ten livestock output categories and seventeen different kinds of inputs were examined. The individual input items are the capital inputs of taxes, interest on debt, machinery expenses, fertilizer and lime, other crop expenses, machinery depreciation, livestock expenses, building repairs, electricity, miscellaneous expenses, building depreciation; improved land (for crops and pasture); individual labour inputs of owner-operator labour, hired labour and unpaid family labour; and additional livestock-feed shipments to Ontario consisting of high energy feed (in spring grains equivalents) and protein supplement (as 44 percent protein soymeal equivalent). The separate quantities

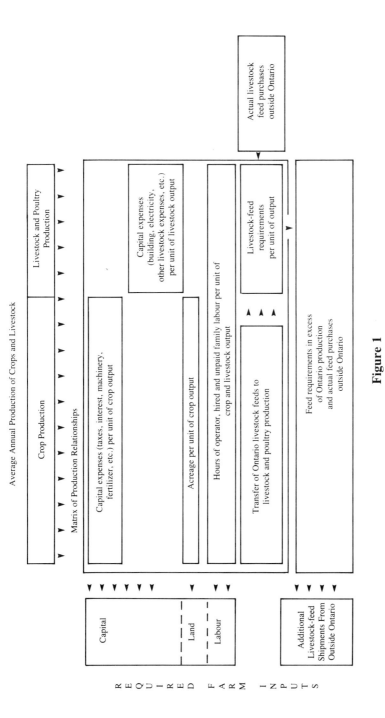

Figure 1

Schematic Diagram of Input Requirement Generator Model of Ontario Agriculture

TABLE 2

AVERAGE 1951 TO 1955 FIXED TECHNOLOGY INPUT-OUTPUT COEFFICIENTS FOR THE INPUT REQUIREMENT GENERATOR MODEL OF ONTARIO AGRICULTURE

Required Farm Inputs		Production Coefficients Per Unit of Crop and Livestock Output																
		Winter Wheat	Spring Grains	Soy-beans	Grain Corn	Fodder Corn	Hay	Seeded Pasture	Potatoes	White Beans	Tobacco	Rye	Buck-wheat	Flax	Tomatoes	Apples	Grapes	Other Crops
		(bushels)	(bushels)	(bushels)	(bushels)	(tons)	(tons)	(acres)	(75 lb bags)	(cwt.)	(green lbs.)	(bushels)	(bushels)	(bushels)	(bushels)	(bushels)	(tons)	(acres)
Capital																		
Taxes on Owned Farmland	Dollars	.0786	.0597	.1591	.0437	.2531	1.3839	.9941	.0172	.5633	.0072	.1210	.1187	.1992	.0371	.0623	4.6526	2.5757
Interest on Indebtedness	Dollars	.0489	.0277	.1433	.0236	.1382	.5684	.6367	.0093	.3377	.0043	.0561	.0551	.0924	.0045	.1341	7.4450	1.6029
Total Machinery Expenses	Dollars	.3345	.1641	.3468	.2210	1.4261	2.6050	0	.1722	1.2274	.0295	.3325	.3262	.5474	.1193	.7087	8.1491	10.9661
Fertilizer and Lime	Dollars	.1012	.0624	.0421	.0839	.3457	.9335	.1171	.1684	.2877	.0113	.1264	.1240	.2081	.0340	.0259	1.2166	3.3186
Other Crop Expenses	Dollars	.0408	.0417	.0638	.0120	.0699	.7909	0	.0341	.2808	.0210	.0845	.0829	.1391	.0249	.2117	1.1842	3.3381
Machinery Depreciation	Dollars	.1845	.0905	.1918	.1222	.7878	1.4406	0	.0951	.6770	.0163	.1833	.1799	.3018	.0659	.3912	4.5025	6.0587
Livestock Expenses	Dollars	0	0	0	0	0	0	0	0	0	0	0	0	0	0	0	0	0
Building Repairs	Dollars	0	0	0	0	0	0	0	0	0	0	0	0	0	0	0	0	0
Electricity & Telephone	Dollars	0	0	0	0	0	0	0	0	0	0	0	0	0	0	0	0	0
Miscellaneous Expenses	Dollars	0	0	0	0	0	0	0	0	0	0	0	0	0	0	0	0	0
Depreciation on Buildings	Dollars	0	0	0	0	0	0	0	0	0	0	0	0	0	0	0	0	0
Land																		
Improved Land	Acres	.0305	.0236	.0433	.0171	.1000	.5076	1.0	.0068	.0935	.0007	.0478	.0469	.0787	.0039	.0089	.4950	1.0

TABLE 2 (Cont'd.)

AVERAGE 1951 TO 1955 FIXED TECHNOLOGY INPUT-OUTPUT COEFFICIENTS FOR THE INPUT REQUIREMENT GENERATOR MODEL OF ONTARIO AGRICULTURE

Labour

	Unit																	
Owner-Operator	Hours	.1929	.1641	.2933	.1313	.7678	2.7511	.9033	.5835	.6334	.2384	.3325	.3262	.5474	.6235	1.4471	80.4825	9.0329
Hired Labour	Hours	.0416	.0354	.0633	.0283	.1656	.5934	.1949	.1259	.1366	.0514	.0717	.0704	.1181	.1345	.3122	17.3612	1.9485
Unpaid Family Labour	Hours	.0875	.0744	.1331	.0596	.3484	1.2482	.4098	.2648	.2874	.1082	.1508	.1480	.2484	.2829	.6566	36.5161	4.0984

Livestock-Feed Transfer Rows

	Unit																	
High Energy Feed Transfer Row (spring grain equivalent)	Pounds	0	36.99	0	65.87	0	0	0	0	0	0	0	0	0	0	0	0	0
Protein Supplement Transfer Row (soymeal 44% protein equivalent)	Pounds	0	0	47.22	0	0	0	0	0	0	0	0	0	0	0	0	0	0
Roughage (alfalfa hay equivalent)	Pounds	0	0	0	0	530.1	2,000	2,378.07	0	0	0	0	0	0	0	0	0	0

Additional Feed Shipments to Ontario

(Domestic and Foreign)

	Unit
High Energy Feed (spring grain equivalent)	Pounds
Protein Supplement (soymeal 44% protein equivalent)	Pounds

TABLE 2 (Cont'd.)
AVERAGE 1951 TO 1955 FIXED TECHNOLOGY INPUT-OUTPUT COEFFICIENTS FOR THE INPUT REQUIREMENT GENERATOR MODEL OF ONTARIO AGRICULTURE

Required Farm Inputs		Production Coefficients Per Unit of Crop and Livestock Output										FEED SHIPMENTS FROM OUTSIDE ONTARIO			Transfer Colums for Additional Livestock-Seed Requirements	
												Actual Livestock-feed Purchases				
		Beef	Veal	Milk	Pork	Chicken	Eggs	Turkey	Geese & Ducks	Mutton & Lamb	Horses	High Energy Feed (pounds)	Protein Supplement (pounds)	High Energy Feed (pounds)	Protein Supplement (pounds)
		(pounds)	(pounds)	(pounds)	(pounds)	(pounds)	(dozen)	(pounds)	(pounds)	(pounds)	(head)				
Capital															
Taxes on Owned Farmland	Dollars	0	0	0	0	0	0	0	0	0	0				
Interest on Indebtedness	Dollars	0	0	0	0	0	0	0	0	0	0				
Total Machinery Expenses	Dollars	0	0	0	0	0	0	0	0	0	0				
Fertilizer and Lime	Dollars	0	0	0	0	0	0	0	0	0	0				
Other Crop Expenses	Dollars	0	0	0	0	0	0	0	0	0	0				
Machinery Depreciation	Dollars	0	0	0	0	0	0	0	0	0	0				
Livestock Expenses	Dollars	.0264	.0041	1.6148	.0100	.0047	.0069	.0072	.0030	.0354	0				
Building Repairs	Dollars	.0277	.0043	1.6929	.0105	.0049	.0073	.0075	.0031	.0371	0				
Electricity & Telephone	Dollars	.0104	.0016	.6379	.0040	.0018	.0027	.0028	.0012	.0140	0				
Miscellaneous Expenses	Dollars	.0372	.0058	2.2728	.0141	.0066	.0097	.0101	.0041	.0498	0				
Depreciation on Buildings	Dollars	.0319	.0050	1.9526	.0121	.0057	.0084	.0087	.0036	.0428	0				
Land															
Improved Land	Acres	0	0	0	0	0	0	0	0	0	0				

TABLE 2 (Cont'd.)

AVERAGE 1951 TO 1955 FIXED TECHNOLOGY INPUT-OUTPUT COEFFICIENTS FOR THE INPUT REQUIREMENT GENERATOR MODEL OF ONTARIO AGRICULTURE

Item	Unit														
Labour															
Owner-Operator	Hours	.3371	.0569	24.5604	.1039	.0604	.0895	.0918	.0423	.4014	0				
Hired Labour	Hours	.0727	.0123	5.2980	.0224	.0130	.0193	.0198	.0091	.0866	0				
Unpaid Family Labour	Hours	.1530	.0258	11.1434	.0471	.0274	.0406	.0417	.0192	.0182	0				
Livestock-Feed Transfer Rows															
High Energy Feed Transfer Row (spring grain equivalent)	Pounds	-11.1509	0	-481.8758	-4.4688	-3.8366	-4.1342	-4.5770	-4.7425	-3.2551	-661.4196	1	0	1	0
Protein Supplement Transfer Row (soymeal 44% protein equivalent)	Pounds	0	-.2378	-33.5291	-.72103	-.9696	.8137	-1.40795	-.8075	0	0	0	1	0	1
Roughage (alfalfa hay equivalent)	Pounds	-38.1241	0	-2154.23	0	0	0	0	0	-26.6261	-8029.2	0	0	0	0
Additional Feed Shipments to Ontario (Domestic and Foreign)															
High Energy Feed (spring grain equivalent)	Pounds											0	0	-1	0
Protein Supplement (soymeal 44% protein equivalent)	Pounds											0	0	0	-1

of the different kinds of inputs per unit of output generated for each kind of crop and livestock activity according to their requirements in the 1951-55 base period are presented in Table 2.

It should be noted that taxes represent a transfer payment and could be excluded as a true input expense. In this study, however, property taxes were included as a crude proxy for infrastructure inputs, since a significant share of property taxes are typically used for roads, electrification and other similar inputs.

Constructing Fixed Technology Input-Output Coefficients

Published statistics of the actual production of crops and livestock and the actual consumption of farm inputs (for the Province of Ontario) in the 1951-55 period were used to construct the input-output coefficients used in the IRGM. The 1951-55 base period data were derived as an average over a five-year period (1951-55) in order to minimize distortions resulting from vagaries of weather, production cycles, price fluctuations, external market disorders and other factors in any given single year.

In calculating input requirements, data were available by aggregate totals for individual inputs, but not available by individual crop and livestock activity. Aggregate input data therefore had to be disaggregated among the total of crops and livestock. For example, aggregate machinery expense, which was one of eleven capital inputs in the IRGM, had to be disaggregated among seventeen different crop activities. Since detailed estimates of the average consumption of individual inputs used to produce each unit of output between 1951 and 1955 were not available, published cost of production and farm management studies of the 1951-55 period were utilized to estimate the distribution of the quantities of inputs used for each specific commodity.

In using the cost of production and farm management studies to provide details on the technology of the 1951-55 era, it was recognized that the studies were not representative of the average farm in Ontario during the period. These studies only represented a sample of the farm technology in use during a certain point in time among cooperating farmers, who often were the more progressive operators. When the production relationships published in the cost of production and farm management studies were used, the IRGM either overestimated or underestimated the aggregate consumption of farm inputs. As a result, it was necessary to make proportional adjustments to these production relationships in order to distribute more accurately the aggregate total of farm inputs actually used among the different crop and livestock activities. In other words, if the aggregate input total actually used in the 1951-55 period was not allocated completely given the 1951-55 production studies coefficients, the coefficients in the model for each commodity were adjusted by the percentage difference between the actual aggregate input total and the aggregate total derived by using the coefficients from the cost of production studies.

While it is conceded that the estimated production relationships may be an imperfect representation of the inputs used on the average farm, the technique does maintain the same relative proportions of inputs used by each crop and livestock activity as was reported in the cost of production studies conducted during this era.

Livestock Feed

The IRGM was operated by first supplying land inputs to produce all horticultural and special crops (tobacco, flax, etc.). The remaining land inputs were used to produce feed requirements necessary for each year's actual production of livestock. All livestock feed supplies actually produced within Ontario each year and the actual imports of livestock feed were assumed to be available as feed for the livestock sector. If additional Ontario livestock feeds were available after the input requirements of the livestock had been satisfied, they were registered as exports. If the internally produced livestock feed supplies were insufficient to meet the livestock production requirements, additional feeds were transferred into the livestock system from external sources and charged as feed brought into Ontario.

Limited Land and Unlimited Land Analysis

The IRGM was designed to consider two alternative situations with regard to the agricultural land available for crop production. In the first computer simulation of the IRGM, the quantity of land was limited to the average acreage in use between 1951 and 1955 (the limited land analysis). If additional supplies of livestock feed were required to maintain the actual livestock production each year between 1956 and 1978, imports of livestock feed were recorded. In the second computer simulation, an unlimited area of land was assumed to be available for use to meet any additional roughage and high energy feed (spring grains) requirements of livestock production. Additional livestock feed imports were limited to protein supplements (soymeal).

ADJUSTING LABOUR INPUTS FOR INCREASED QUALITY DUE TO HIGHER GENERAL EDUCATION

The improved productivity of agricultural labour due to higher general education (which was not included as an investment expense) was accounted for by adjusting the fixed technology labour requirements downward by a measure of the percentage increase in years of schooling among farmers. Since few data are available for Canada on the impact of general education on agricultural labour productivity, two alternative adjustments were used to depict different educational effects. The first adjustment consisted of reducing the fixed technology labour hours each year by one-half of the percentage increase in average years of schooling (to reflect a less than proportional impact on agricultural productivity), while the second utilized an equal percentage reduction. Over the 1951 to 1978 time period, average years of schooling increased by an estimated 26.36 percent. This resulted in a 13.18 percent reduction in fixed technology labour requirements by 1978 under the one-half percentage increase adjustment, and a 26.36 reduction under the equal percentage increase adjustment. These adjustments had the impact of reducing the amount of inputs saved and therefore reduced the reported returns from agricultural research and supporting services.

CALCULATING THE VALUE OF INPUTS SAVED

The actual inputs used were subtracted from the hypothetical required inputs to calculate the inputs saved by agricultural research. The hypothetical inputs of land, labour and additional livestock feed imports required from 1956 to 1978, using the base period technology of the IRGM, were expressed in physical units. The hypothetical capital inputs required were expressed in constant 1951-55 dollar values. They were inflated to nominal prices (from 1956 to 1978) using individual farm input price indexes for each capital input before subtracting the value of the capital inputs (expressed in nominal dollars) actually used each year.

In order to aggregate the inputs saved by agricultural research, the savings in inputs of land, labour and livestock feed imports had to be converted to monetary values. Labour hours saved were priced at their opportunity cost. Operator labour hours saved were priced at the wages of non-farm labour, and hired farm labour and unpaid family labour hours saved were priced at the hired farm labour wage. An imputed rent was calculated for land savings. Imported livestock feed saved was priced at the annual CIF price of feed imported into Ontario.

The total value of inputs saved was calculated by summing up the dollar savings for each individual input for each year and converting the 1956 to 1978 yearly totals to constant 1978 prices using the Consumer Price Index. The future benefits extending from 1979 to 1998 were then added to this figure by depreciating the 1978 annual benefits by 5 percent each year, because it was assumed that there would be a continual decline in annual benefits from 1978 to a zero level in twenty years, if all research was ceased in 1972.

A summary of the overall benefits from agricultural research and supporting services is presented in Table 3 under the limited land analysis with a 50 percent schooling increase adjustment rate for labour. Total benefits amounted to $2.7 billion in 1978 alone, $46 billion from 1956 to 1978, and are projected to reach $73.2 billion by 1998 in continuing benefits from the 1950 to 1972 research expenditures.

In general, agricultural research has led to the substitution of capital inputs for labour and land. From 1956 to 1978, cumulative capital costs increased over the 1951-55 fixed technology level by nearly $7.4 billion and are projected to reach $14.6 billion by 1998. Of the capital inputs, only property taxes and building repairs are projected to be lower than under fixed technology because of fewer land acres and building repairs required with research advances. Labour inputs, on the other hand, were reduced tremendously and represent the primary source of benefits. Labour input savings amounted to $44.4 billion cumulatively from 1956 to 1978 and are projected at $72.3 billion by 1998.

Land savings represented cumulative benefits of only $1.4 billion by 1978 and a projected overall benefit of $3.2 billion by 1998. This figure is misleading,

TABLE 3

**SUMMARY OF INPUTS SAVED IN ONTARIO AGRICULTURAL
PRODUCTION FROM RESEARCH IMPROVEMENTS, 1956-1998**
(Constant 1978 Dollar Values)[a]

Inputs	1978	1956-1978	1956-1998
Capital:			
Taxes	32,654,000	561,251,000	887,788,000
Interest	-139,290,000	-1,205,976,000	-2,598,873,000
Machinery Expenses	-58,796,000	-1,406,527,000	-1,994,487,000
Fertilizers	-110,645,000	-1,272,309,000	-2,378,757,000
Other Crop Expenses	-96,914,000	-1,489,671,000	-2,458,805,000
Machinery Depreciation	-152,652,000	-1,212,641,000	-2,739,157,000
Other Livestock Expenses	-175,501,000	-1,108,576,000	-2,863,582,000
Building Repairs	70,103,000	592,816,000	1,293,845,000
Electricity	-25,905,000	-145,532,000	-404,577,000
Miscellaneous Expenses	-50,504,000	-468,685,000	-973,723,000
Building Depreciation	-11,169,000	-242,296,000	-353,988,000
Capital Subtotal	$-718,619,000	$-7,398,146,000	$-14,584,316,000
Land:			
Physical ('000 acres)	1,755,000	27,604,000	45,153,000
Value	$178,222,000	$1,418,545,000	$3,200,759,000
Labour:			
Operator Hours ('000)	268,000	5,264,000	7,942,000
Value	1,812,840,000	30,726,399,000	48,854,741,000
Unpaid Family Hours ('000)	207,000	2,852,000	5,908,000
Value	774,422,000	11,574,121,000	19,318,332,000
Hired Labour Hours ('000)	56,000	676,000	1,235,000
Value	198,561,000	2,091,362,000	4,076,967,000
Labour Subtotal	$2,785,823,000	$44,391,882,000	$72,250,040,000
Additional Feed Imports:			
Energy Feeds			
Tons	5,848,000	83,864,000	142,345,000
Value	490,097,000	7,834,686,000	12,735,649,000
Protein Feeds			
Tons	-74,000	-1,182,000	-1,918,000
Value	-16,388,000	-252,087,000	-415,963,000
Additional Feed Import Subtotal	$473,709,000	$7,582,599,000	$12,319,686,000
Total Value of Inputs Saved	$2,719,135,000	$45,994,880,000	$73,186,169,000

[a] Limited land analysis with labour adjusted for increases in quality by one-half the percentage increase in average years of general education by farmers.

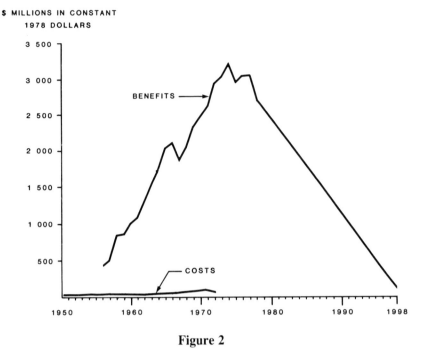

Figure 2

Costs and Benefits of Agricultural Research and Supporting Services in Ontario, 1950 - 1998 (Limited Land Analysis and Labour Quality Adjustment at One-Half the Rate of Increase in Years of General Education)

however, because the available land was limited to the 1951-55 average culti-vated acreage. Ontario would not have had enough land to produce its food under the 1951-55 technology and would have required an additional cumulative $12.3 billion in feed imports by 1998. To produce Ontario's actual food amounts under 1951-55 technology without additional feed imports would have required 7.8 million hectares of land in 1978, compared with the 4.1 million hectares which were actually under crops and pasture at that time.

The overall relationship between benefits and investment costs in agricultural research and supporting services is presented in Figure 2. This figure illustrates the "mountain" of benefits compared to a very low relative level of costs.

RETURNS TO AGRICULTURAL RESEARCH AND SUPPORTING SERVICES

The returns to agriculture research and supporting services in Ontario relative to investment costs were measured both as a Benefit/Cost (B/C) ratio and as an Internal Rate of Return (IRR). Benefit/Cost ratios and Internal Rates of Return use identical cost and benefit data. However, they use different procedures for discounting these data to a common base year, and therefore provide different measurements of returns. The Benefit/Cost ratio may be interpreted as a measure of the additional benefits of an investment that are returned after compensation has been made for the use of capital at some appropriate interest rate. If society were satisfied to obtain a breakeven position on its investment (i.e., a return that would just compensate for the cost of borrowed capital), then a B/C ratio of 1:1 would just meet this requirement. Any B/C ratio above the 1:1 level would indicate a net gain of social benefits.

The Internal Rate of Return (IRR) is the single rate of discount that will just equate discounted benefits and costs. It may be interpreted as the compound rate of interest earned on an investment, or as the rate of interest return that could be derived from each dollar invested, from the date of its expenditure. In this study the IRR was calculated by using an iterative procedure in which the benefits and costs were discounted at different rates of interest until the sum of the present value of the benefits equaled the sum of the present value of the costs.

MEASUREMENT OF RETURNS

In this study the most realistic conditions for measuring returns were considered to be (1) the limited land analysis, (2) adjustments to labour productivity for general education at a percentage reduction in fixed technology labour hours equal to one-half the percentage increase in average years of general education completed by farmers, and (3) a real discount rate of 2 percent.[3] Under these conditions, the overall Benefit/Cost ratio was *37.4:1* and the Internal Rate of Return *65.7 percent* per year.

These measurements of returns are extremely high and indicate that agricultural research and supporting services are some of the best public investments available today. The B/C ratio of 37.4 to 1, for example, is many times greater than typical ratios for public investments in infrastructure of 0.5 to 1 (losing money) up to 1.5 to 1. Furthermore, it should be recognized that the benefits of agricultural research and supporting services are some of the most widely distributed and progressive of all public benefits. By reducing the inputs and costs required in food production, all consumers of food benefit. These benefits also represent a proportionally greater improvement in the welfare of poor people than the rich, since the poor spend relatively greater amounts of their income on food than the rich. Ontario farmers have also benefited by maintaining their competitiveness with producers in other provinces and countries, as well as benefiting from such changes as the improvement in working conditions through the development of labour saving technology and the reduction in manual labour requirements.

SENSITIVITY ANALYSIS OF RETURNS

The sensitivity of the returns measurements is analyzed under a variety of different conditions for land availability, general education, labour productivity adjustments, discount rates and research time lags in Tables 4-6. Under all conditions, the limited land analysis generates lower measurements than the unlimited land analysis, with B/C ratios ranging from six to eleven points lower and IRRs about 2 percent lower under equal other conditions. Benefit/Cost ratios are sensitive to increasing interest discount rates from 1 to 5 percent, decreasing the ratios from 41.9 to 27.5 under the limited land and one-half general education labour quality adjustments. Benefit/Cost ratios are also sensitive to changes in adjustment for general education effects on labour productivity (ranging from four to seven points per change), but are relatively insensitive to changes in the research time lag. Internal Rate of Return calculations, on the other hand, are sensitive primarily to research time lag lengths, with only small changes for land availability and general education labour productivity adjustments. Under all the conditions examined, however, it should be noted that the Benefit/Cost ratios and Internal Rates of Returns were extremely high (with a low B/C ratio of 23.6 to 1 and a low IRR of 54.5 percent), identifying agricultural research and supporting services as one of the highest payoff investments available today. These results are also consistent with the high rates of return to agricultural research found in other studies (Ruttan, 1978).

FUTURE BENEFITS

Future benefits of agricultural research in Ontario will depend on many factors. The most important consideration will be the amount of research activity and, therefore, the level of research funding.

Several projections of future benefits, indicating the effect of different funding levels for research and supporting services, are shown in Figure 3 and summarized in Table 7. Actual funding levels are shown through 1980, with alternative projected levels from 1981 onward. All benefits are projected at the same rate of return per dollar of expenditure experienced in the 1950 to 1978 period. Benefits are projected to start six years after expenditures and to continue for approximately twenty years.

A steady rise in benefits under all alternatives is indicated until around 1990 because research recently finished or underway will provide increasing returns through the 1980s. A complete suspension of research funding after 1980, however, would have caused benefits to start declining sharply in 1989, reaching zero by the year 2005. Maintaining funding levels at the 1980 dollar amounts would allow a slight increase until 1991, but after that date inflation would cause sharp declines in benefits by reducing the real level of expenditures. These two examples illustrate the need for adequate research support just to maintain the present level of benefits.

Increasing expenditures at the rate of inflation would generate higher benefits, but these would eventually level out (shown in Figure 3 as $4.3 billion a year by 2001) without further increases as the backlog of current research benefits is used up. Continually increasing benefits, on the other hand, would require expenditures in excess of the rate of inflation. The 3 percent increase rate above inflation,

TABLE 4

BENEFIT/COST RATIOS OF 1950/51-1972/73 EXPENDITURES IN ONTARIO ON AGRICULTURAL RESEARCH, EXTENSION AND EDUCATION BY THE FEDERAL AND ONTARIO GOVERNMENTS AND PRIVATE AGRICULTURAL INPUT SUPPLY FIRMS, UNDER ALTERNATIVE REAL RATES OF INTEREST DISCOUNT AND ADJUSTMENTS FOR LABOUR PRODUCTIVITY FROM GENERAL EDUCATION

Real Rate of Interest Discount on Investment	Limited Land Analysis[a] Benefit/Cost Ratios: assuming alternative rates of increase in agricultural labour productivity due to increased levels of general education			Unlimited Land Analysis[b] Benefit/Cost Ratios: assuming alternative rates of increase in agricultural labour productivity due to increased levels of general education		
(%)	A	B	C	A	B	C
1	49.0	41.9	34.7	60.2	52.5	44.7
2	43.5	37.4	31.3	53.1	46.5	39.9
3	38.8	33.6	28.4	47.1	41.5	35.8
4	34.8	30.3	25.8	42.0	37.2	32.3
5	31.4	27.5	23.6	37.7	33.5	29.3

[a] The Ontario Land Base is limited (to the acreage available in 1951-55); all additional feed requirements above observed shipments were assumed to be imported.

[b] All feed supplies are assumed to be grown in Ontario on additional land above that in use in 1951-55.

A - Productivity of labour is unchanged by general education.

B - Productivity of labour increases at one-half the rate of increase of general education.

C - Productivity of labour increases at the same rate as the increase in general education.

TABLE 5

BENEFIT/COST RATIOS OF 1950/51-1972/73 EXPENDITURES IN ONTARIO ON AGRICULTURAL RESEARCH, EXTENSION AND EDUCATION BY THE FEDERAL AND ONTARIO GOVERNMENTS AND PRIVATE AGRICULTURAL INPUT SUPPLY FIRMS, UNDER A 2 PERCENT REAL RATE OF DISCOUNT, ALTERNATIVE RESEARCH TIME LAGS AND ADJUSTMENTS FOR LABOUR PRODUCTIVITY FROM GENERAL EDUCATION

Research Time Lag[c] Assumed (years)	Limited Land Analysis[a] Benefit/Cost Ratios: assuming alternative rates of increase in agricultural labour productivity due to increased levels of general education			Unlimited Land Analysis[b] Benefit/Cost Ratios: assuming alternative rates of increase in agricultural labour productivity due to increased levels of general education		
	A	B	C	A	B	C
5	44.4	38.1	31.9	54.2	47.5	40.7
6	43.5	37.4	31.3	53.1	46.5	39.9
7	42.6	36.6	30.7	52.0	45.6	39.1

a The Ontario Land Base is limited (to the acreage available in 1951-55); all additional feed requirements above observed shipments were assumed to be imported.

b All feed supplies are assumed to be grown in Ontario on additional land above that in use in 1951-55.

c The benefits from 1956 to 1998 were assumed to occur between 1955 and 1997 for the five-year research time lag and to occur between 1957 and 1999 for the seven-year research time lag.

A - Productivity of labour is unchanged by general education.

B - Productivity of labour increases at one-half the rate of increase of general education.

C - Productivity of labour increases at the same rate as the increase in general education.

TABLE 6

ANNUAL INTERNAL RATE OF RETURN TO 1950/51-1972/73 EXPENDITURES IN ONTARIO ON
AGRICULTURAL RESEARCH, EXTENSION AND EDUCATION BY THE FEDERAL AND ONTARIO
GOVERNMENTS AND PRIVATE AGRICULTURAL INPUT SUPPLY FIRMS, UNDER ALTERNATIVE
RESEARCH TIME LAGS AND ADJUSTMENTS FOR LABOUR PRODUCTIVITY
FROM GENERAL EDUCATION

Research Time Lag Assumed[c]	Limited Land Analysis[a] Annual Internal Rate of Return (%): assuming alternative rates of increase in agricultural labour productivity due to increased levels of general education			Unlimited Land Analysis[b] Annual Internal Rate of Return (%): assuming alternative rates of increase in agricultural labour productivity due to increased levels of general education		
(years)	A	B	C	A	B	C
5	82.3	81.8	81.3	84.6	84.1	83.6
6	66.2	65.7	65.3	68.0	67.6	67.1
7	55.4	55.0	54.5	57.0	56.5	56.1

[a] The Ontario Land Base is limited (to the acreage available in 1951-55); all additional feed requirements above observed shipments were assumed to be imported.

[b] All feed supplies are assumed to be grown in Ontario on additional land above that in use in 1951-55.

[c] The benefits from 1956 to 1998 were assumed to occur from 1955 to 1997 for the five-year research time lag, and from 1957 to 1999 for the seven-year research time lag.

A - Productivity of labour is unchanged by general education.

B - Productivity of labour increases at one-half the rate of increase of general education.

C - Productivity of labour increases at the same rate as the increase in general education.

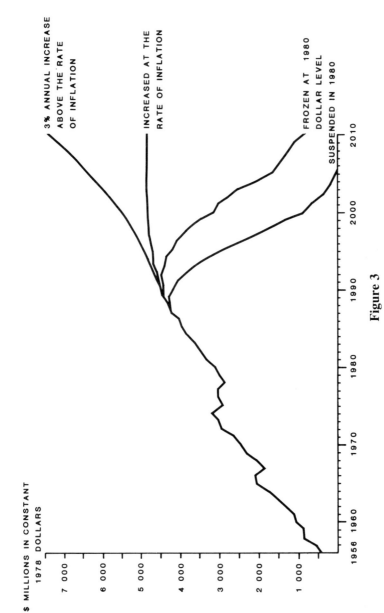

Figure 3

Benefits in Ontario of Expenditures from 1950 - 1980 on Agricultural
Research and Supporting Services and Projections of Benefits to the Year
2010 under Alternative Levels of Expenditures on Agricultural Research
and Supporting Services from 1981 - 2000

TABLE 7

ACTUAL AND PROJECTED BENEFITS OF EXPENDITURES ON AGRICULTURAL RESEARCH
AND SUPPORTING SERVICES IN ONTARIO UNTIL 2010 UNDER EXISTING EXPENDITURES
AND ALTERNATIVE EXPENDITURE LEVELS FROM 1981 TO 2000
(in millions of 1978 constant dollars)

| Year | Benefits from Expenditures on Research and Supporting Services[a] 1950-1980 | Year | Projected Benefits under Alternative Patterns of Expenditures[b] 1981-2000 | | | |
			(1) Expenditures Suspended in 1980	(2) Expenditures Frozen in 1980	(3) Expenditures Increased at Rate of Inflation	(4) Expenditures Increased at 3% Above Inflation
1956	$ 433	1987	$4200	$4220	$4235	$4240
57	553	88	4275	4315	4320	4325
58	857	89	4300	4430	4435	4435
59	866	1990	4185	4440	4490	4510
1960	1040	91	4030	4480	4570	4600
61	1126	92	3900	4475	4615	4690
62	1327	93	3640	4415	4680	4760
63	1539	94	3355	4370	4710	4840
64	1750	95	2980	4225	4720	4935
65	2056	96	2580	4120	4765	5040
66	2116	97	2120	3940	4795	5145
67	1872	98	1710	3750	4815	5265
68	2075	99	1325	3495	4820	5385
69	2338	2000	895	3145	4830	5535
1970	2474	01	725	3040	4845	5690
71	2638	02	480	2775	4845	5855
72	2943	03	290	2545	4845	6020
73	3037	04	145	2095	4845	6200
74	3201	05	50	1710	4845	6385
75	2949	06	0	1540	4845	6575
76	3035	07	0	1395	4845	6772
77	3050	08	0	1250	4845	6975
78	2719	09	0	1120	4845	7185
79	3030	2010	0	900	4845	7400
1980	3125					
81	3345					
82	3480					
83	3635					
84	3810					
85	3940					
86	4025					

[a] Based on actual expenditures through 1978 with 1979 and 1980 expenditures assumed at the 1978 level. Returns to expenditures beyond 1972 were projected with a six-year lag between expenditures and benefits and calculated at the same rate as occurred on expenditures over the 1950 to 1972 period.

[b] Assumed inflation rate of 11 percent.

as illustrated, provides increases in total benefits at approximately the same rate experienced since 1956.

The financial commitment to agricultural research and supporting services in the past has been very important in keeping Canadians well fed at one of the most reasonable food costs in the world. With an increasing population and limited land base, new technology remains the most important method of ensuring an internationally competitive Ontario food and agricultural system.

Given the high return on investment and widespread distribution of benefits, agricultural research and supporting services warrant top priority for strong financial support in the future.

NOTES

1. For a more complete analysis of the study findings, data sources and proce-
    dures see Barry E. Prentice and George L. Brinkman, *The Value of Agricul-
    tural Research in Ontario: Research Methodology, Data Sources, and Princi-
    pal Findings*, AEEE Publication 82/9 (School of Agricultural Economics
    and Extension Education, University of Guelph, July 1982).

2. For example, Harosoy, a soybean variety developed at the Harrow Research
    Station in the 1950s, became the major soybean variety grown in the United
    States during the mid-1960s. At that time, about half the Mid-West soybean
    growing area (approximately 3,200,000 ha) was planted to Harosoy, yielding
    60 to 120 kg/ha more than the best U.S. soybean variety. Several major
    soybean varieties grown today still have Canadian Harosoy in their parentage.

3. The limited land analysis was chosen because of the physical limitations
    on land and of the unlikely prospect of bringing into production the large
    quantity of new land required under the alternative unlimited land analysis.
    The labour adjustment for general education was based on the premise that
    general education would improve the productivity of agricultural labour at
    a rate less than the rate of increase in general educational levels because
    only a portion of the general education would provide direct benefits in agri-
    culture. The real discount rate of 2 percent was chosen to reflect the social
    opportunity cost of public expenditures over the period. Unfortunately, no
    appropriate studies measuring the real returns to public expenditures over
    the time period analyzed in this study were available. However, the presence
    of low real rates of return in recent years in the private sector and the far
    greater use of public than private funds for transfers instead of output-
    generating investments would suggest that a 2 percent rate should be adequate.
    As an example, the Farm Credit Corporation real lending rate, from December
    1963 to December 1981, averaged about 2.2 percent.

REFERENCES

Prentice, Barry E., and George L. Brinkman. *The Value of Agricultural Research
    in Ontario: Research Methodology, Data Sources, and Principal Findings.*
    AEEE Publication 82/9. School of Agricultural Economics and Extension
    Education, University of Guelph, July 1982.

Receiver General of Canada. *Public Accounts of Canada.* Ottawa, Canada: Min-
    istry of Supply and Services Canada, annual.

Ruttan, Vernon W. *Bureaucratic Productivity: The Case of Agricultural Research.*
    Staff Paper P78-16. Dept. of Agricultural and Applied Economics, University
    of Minnesota, November 1978.

Treasurer of Ontario and Minister of Economics. *Ontario Public Accounts.* Toronto,
    Ontario: Ministry of Treasury and Economics, annual.

APPENDIX A

CALCULATION PROCEDURES FOR MEASURING BENEFITS FROM ONTARIO AGRICULTURAL RESEARCH

Research benefits are represented by

$$\sum_{t=1}^{i} \left[VX_{ft,t} - VX_{q,t} \right] plus \sum_{t^*=1}^{i} URB_{t}^*$$

where

VX_{ft} = Aggregate value of inputs required to produce Ontario's actual output of agricultural production under 1951-1955 average fixed technology

VX_{a} = Aggregate value of actual inputs used each year to produce Ontario's actual output of agricultural production

t = 1956 to 1978

URB = Undepreciated remaining benefits per year from existing research that would continue beyond 1978 into the future (from 1979 to 1998)

t^* = 1979 to 1998

Total research benefits were calculated as follows:

(1)   Yearly Benefits

For capital inputs

$$BX_{i,t} = \sum_{j=1}^{c} \left[P_{i,t} \cdot FT_{i,j,t} \right] - VA_{i,t}$$

For land, labour and feed imports

$$BX_{i,t} = P_{i,t} \sum_{j=1}^{c} \left[FT_{i,j,t} - A_{i,t} \right]$$

where

BX_{i} = Benefits per type of inputs per year (from 1956-1978)

P = Annual average price of each input per year

FT = Quantities of each type of input required under average 1951-55 base year technology to generate the actual production of each individual agricultural commodity each year

A   = Quantities of each type of input (for land, labour and food imports) actually used in aggregate to produce the actual aggregate production of all crops and livestock in Ontario each year

VA   = Aggregate value of each type of input (for capital inputs only) actually used to produce the actual aggregate Ontario production

c   = Agricultural commodities, consisting of seventeen crop and ten livestock activities

X_i = Types of inputs, with

X_i(Capital)   = a. Taxes on farmland
                        b. Interest on indebtedness
                        c. Total machinery expenses
                        d. Fertilizer and lime
                        e. Other crop expenses
                        f. Machinery depreciation
                        g. Livestock expenses
                        h. Building repairs
                        i. Electricity and telephone
                        j. Miscellaneous expenses
                        k. Building depreciation

Physical quantities of fixed technology (FT) capital inputs were measured in terms of 1951-55 average dollar units, while actual (A) capital inputs were measured only in value terms (VA).

X_i(land)   = acres of land
X_i(labour)   = hours of work by
                        a. Farm operators
                        b. Hired labourers
                        c. Unpaid family help

X_i(feed imports)   = pounds of imported energy and protein feeds needed to meet any shortfall in production under fixed technology, measured in terms of equivalents of
                        a. soybean meal
                        b. corn

PX_i for individual FT capital inputs per year were represented by farm input price indexes adjusted to the 1951-55 base year average valued as 100.

PX_i for FT and A land, labour and import inputs were as follows:

PX_i land   = Imputed annual rental value calculated as the prime interest rate times the current market value of land and buildings per acre

PX$_i$ labour   = Operator wages calculated as the average Ontario hourly manufacturing wage per year plus 5 percent for management contributions. Hired and unpaid family wages calculated as the average hourly hired agricultural wage rate (without board) per year

PX$_i$ imports   = Price of corn at Chicago plus freight and price of soybeans at Decatur, Illinois plus freight

$$(2) \quad BY_i = \sum_{i=1}^{n} BX_{i,t}$$

where

BY = Benefits per year from all inputs

(3)   RBY$_1$ = BY adjusted to constant 1978 dollars by the CPI

$$(4) \quad TB = \sum_{t=1956}^{1978} RBY_t + \sum_{t^*=1979}^{1998} URB_{t^*}$$

where

$$UDB_{t^*} = RBY_{1978}\left[1-.05(t^*-1978)\right]$$

(5)

$$\text{Discounted TB} = \sum_{t=1956}^{1978} \frac{RBY_t}{(1+r)^{t-1950}} + \sum_{t^*=1979}^{1998} \frac{URB_{t^*}}{(1+r)^{t^*-1950}}$$

where

r = discount factor

CHAPTER 9

PUBLIC AND PRIVATE RETURNS FROM JOINT VENTURE RESEARCH IN AGRICULTURE: THE CASE OF MALTING BARLEY

Alvin Ulrich, Hartley Furtan and Andrew Schmitz

In the last decade numerous studies have been conducted in an attempt to estimate the public rate of return that society has enjoyed as a result of public investments in agricultural research.[1] In almost all cases the estimated internal rates have been high relative to returns from other social and private investments.

Studies have also been carried out to estimate the private and public rates of return to private investments in the research and development of new industrial products and processes.[2] Two main points emerge from these latter class of studies: (1) there is almost always a social gain from private investment in R&D, and (2) the social rate of return is usually larger than the private return on private investment.[3]

Most agricultural research is funded solely by public (i.e., government) institutions; a lesser amount is funded solely by private firms.[4] However, there is an additional amount of agricultural research that is conducted and funded jointly by a combination of public institutions and private firms.[5] This paper attempts to estimate the effects of one such jointly-funded agricultural research project. In an era of government budgetary cuts, such jointly-funded projects may become increasingly common as public research institutions seek increasing amounts of private funding.

Few studies have looked at the economic incentives and consequences of such jointly funded research. For instance, is there any incentive for private firms to invest in agricultural research if they cannot patent or copyright their findings? Would society be better off if private firms were not involved at all? How easily, and to what extent, is increased private funding likely to take place? In the past, what have been the results of jointly-funded agricultural research? This study, based on work by Ulrich (1983), is intended to help fill this gap in the literature by examining the results of the jointly-funded development of new Canadian malting barley varieties.

BACKGROUND

Since the 1880s the Canadian government (via Agriculture Canada research stations and university Plant Science departments) has conducted barley variety research. Until the 1940s, barley breeders devoted most of their efforts to developing varieties of barley that were higher yielding, more pest resistant and easier to harvest.

Meanwhile, Canada's major malting firm, Canada Malting Co., began an active extension and pure variety seed distribution program to stimulate increased production of barley with desirable malting characteristics. In 1948, this effort was further enhanced when the other Canadian malting and brewing companies joined with Canada Malting Co. to form the Brewing and Malting Barley Research Institute (BMBRI). This Institute's efforts included: (1) performing small scale malting and brewing trials, (2) coordinating and publicizing results of commercial malting and brewing trials of new varieties, and (3) giving grants to barley breeders to encourage more research and development of better malting barley varieties.

Since that time, twenty-nine new barley varieties have been released (thirteen of which were licensed for malting purposes). Canadian malting barley consumption has doubled, the percentage of total barley acreage planted to malting varieties has gone from 40 to 75 percent, the quality of Canadian malting barley has noticeably improved and Canada has become one of the world's major producers and exporters of barley, malting barley and malt.

The basic malting process consists of allowing barley to germinate for sufficient time to allow the enzymes and starches in the kernel to change from their dormant form to their growing form. Once this happens the barley is heat-treated so that all growth stops. The resultant biologically-dead barley is referred to as malt. This malt is subsequently purchased and used by brewers to make the mash that is used to brew beer.

Although any barley could be brewed to make beer, the present state of industrial and chemical facilities in modern malt and brew houses has ruled out the use of all but the highest quality production from a few, specific barley varieties. These varieties are referred to as malting barleys, to differentiate their potentially different end-use from that of feed barleys, which are used solely for animal feed.

Malting varieties usually have faster, more even germination, lower protein and higher levels of desirable enzymes and starches than do feed varieties. Present malting and brewing technology dictates that malting barleys can be used for feed, but feed barleys cannot be used for malting. Any barley used for malting purposes will sell at a premium over the same barley used for livestock feed even though it is of the identical variety and quality.

Presently, in Canada, about 75 percent of total barley production is produced from barley varieties suitable for malting. Once a farmer actually plants a malting variety he must wait until harvest to see if weather conditions and other agronomic influences have favoured the production of high quality barley. Any barley not selected by malsters for malting purposes must be sold for feed, regardless of its quality. Hence, a farmer has no way of knowing, at planting time, if his production from a malting barley variety will actually be sold for malting or not. Historically, from 10-40 percent of all malting barley variety production is actually sold for malting purposes. Figure 1 gives a diagrammatic representation of the end-use pattern for Canadian barley. Tables 1 and 2 present some historical data on Canadian barley and malting barley production.

From Table 1 we see that Canadian production of all barley has increased about 308.7 percent between 1951 and 1981. During this same period, barley acreage increased by about 175.9 percent and yield per acre by about 175.8 percent.[6]

Table 2 presents data on Canadian malting barley. To get an indication of the *potential* malting barley[7] available, the percent of total barley acres seeded to

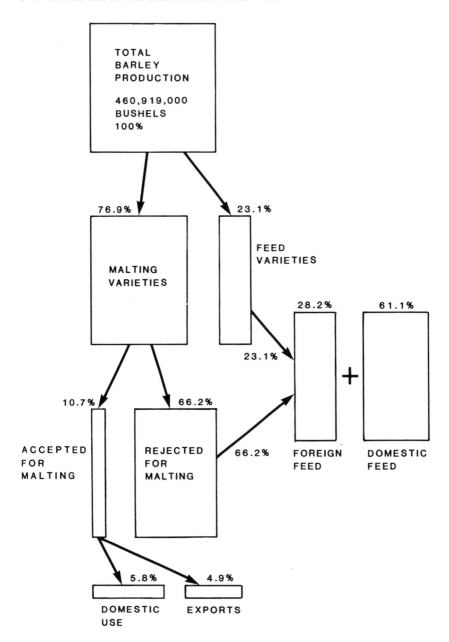

Figure 1

Diagrammatic Representation of End-Use of Canada's Barley Production[1]

---

[1] Percentage figures are based on the average of 1979 - 1981 data. They represent the portion of total production going to a particular use (boxes are drawn to scale).

TABLE 1

HISTORICAL BARLEY STATISTICS, CANADA, 1951-1981

Year	Acres[1] ('000)	All Barley Average Yield[1] (bu./ac.)	Total Production[1] ('000,000 bu.)	% of Acres Planted to Malting Varieties[2]	Potential Malting Barley Production[3] ('000,000 bu.)	Average All Barley Price[4] ($/bu.)	Average Malting Barley Price[5] ($/bu.)
1951	6,510	25.7	167.5	62.5	104.7	1.13	1.24
1952	7,840	31.3	245.4	63.5	155.9	1.10	1.24
1953	8,478	34.4	292.6	65.2	190.1	1.06	1.23
1954	8,908	29.4	262.1	65.0	170.4	.86	.98
1955	7,842	22.3	175.2	59.6	104.4	.89	1.09
1956	9,887	25.4	251.1	65.5	164.5	.87	1.02
1957	8,390	32.1	269.1	72.9	196.1	.79	1.03
1958	9,404	23.0	216.0	76.8	165.9	.76	1.19
1959	9,286	25.6	237.8	78.1	185.7	.77	1.12
1960	7,886	27.3	215.6	78.1	168.4	.74	1.12
1961	6,857	28.2	193.5	79.7	154.2	.80	1.18
1962	5,529	20.4	112.6	77.3	87.1	1.05	1.41
1963	5,287	31.4	165.9	80.0	132.7	.94	1.26
1964	6,177	35.8	221.2	77.0	170.4	.94	1.28
1965	5,495	30.7	168.5	71.5	120.5	1.00	1.36
1966	6,121	35.7	218.3	76.0	165.9	1.03	1.44
1967	7,461	39.7	296.2	80.5	238.5	1.05	1.43
1968	8,121	31.1	252.0	81.6	206.3	.87	1.35
1969	8,854	36.8	326.0	80.6	262.8	.82	1.22
1970	9,358	39.7	371.3	78.5	291.5	.67	1.22
1971	9,894	41.3	408.3	76.8	313.6	.75	1.30
1972	13,981	43.0	601.6	73.8	444.0	.69	1.25
1973	12,509	41.4	518.3	71.8	372.2	1.25	2.45
1974	11,958	39.3	469.6	71.0	333.4	2.50	3.40
1975	11,800	34.3	404.3	71.4	288.7	2.21	3.80
1976	11,041	39.6	437.3	73.3	320.2	2.31	3.35
1977	10,758	44.9	482.9	75.4	364.1	1.92	2.92
1978	11,739	46.2	541.9	77.1	417.8	1.64	2.50
1979	10,533	45.3	477.1	77.0	367.4	1.74	3.15
1980	9,200	42.2	388.6	77.2	300.0	2.33	4.14
1981	11,453	45.2	517.1	76.4	395.1	3.07	4.49

[1] Statistics Canada, *Field Crop Reporting Series* (Cat. No. 22-201), various years.

[2] Estimated by the Brewing and Malting Barley Research Institute.

[3] Col. 5 = Col. 3 times Col. 4.

[4] Statistics Canada, *Grain Trade of Canada* (Cat. No. 32-206), various years.

[5] Canada Malting Co. estimated average annual plant cost of malting barley.

TABLE 2

HISTORICAL CANADIAN MALTING BARLEY POTENTIAL SUPPLY AND DISAPPEARANCE, 1951-1981

Year	Total Domestic Use[1] ('000,000 bu.)	Malt Exports[2] ('000,000 bu.)	Malting Barley Exports[3] ('000,000 bu.)	Total Disappear- ance[4] ('000,000 bu.)	Potential Malting Barley Production[5] ('000,000 bu.)	Use/ Potential Supply Ratio[6]
1951	14.3	3.7	16.3	34.3	104.7	.33
1952	15.1	3.5	16.3	34.9	155.9	.22
1953	15.2	3.3	28.4	46.9	190.1	.25
1954	14.7	4.0	39.8	58.5	170.4	.34
1955	15.2	3.9	23.9	43.0	104.4	.41
1956	15.2	4.3	34.6	54.2	164.5	.33
1957	16.1	4.9	23.1	44.1	196.1	.23
1958	15.2	5.6	28.4	49.2	165.9	.30
1959	16.3	5.9	20.8	43.0	185.7	.23
1960	16.8	6.2	22.0	45.0	168.4	.27
1961	16.9	4.4	18.8	40.1	154.2	.26
1962	17.9	4.3	14.1	35.3	87.1	.42
1963	18.4	3.6	8.3	30.3	132.7	.23
1964	18.9	3.9	15.6	38.4	170.4	.23
1965	19.6	3.2	14.1	36.9	120.5	.31
1966	20.3	3.4	9.5	33.2	165.9	.20
1967	20.6	4.1	11.3	35.9	238.5	.15
1968	20.1	3.8	8.1	32.1	206.3	.16
1969	21.1	3.9	12.0	36.9	262.8	.14
1970	21.5	4.7	17.9	44.1	291.5	.15
1971	23.0	5.5	21.5	50.0	313.6	.16
1972	24.7	5.5	19.0	49.2	444.0	.11
1973	24.7	6.3	19.4	50.5	372.2	.14
1974	25.8	6.2	17.8	49.8	333.4	.15
1975	25.5	7.2	20.2	53.0	288.7	.18
1976	24.8	5.2	20.4	50.3	320.2	.16
1977	25.3	7.2	14.7	47.1	364.1	.13
1978	25.3	9.5	19.6	54.4	417.8	.13
1979	26.8	10.9	14.1	51.8	367.4	.14
1980	27.0	10.8	13.0	50.8	300.0	.17
1981	26.7	10.8	8.3	45.8	395.1	.12

[1] Annual totals are the sum of amounts found in Statistics Canada, *Breweries* (Cat. No. 32-205), *Distilleries* (Cat. No. 32-206) and *Grain Trade of Canada* (Cat. No. 32-206), various years.

[2] Statistics Canada, *Exports* (Cat. No. 65-202), various years.

[3] Estimated by the Brewing and Malting Barley Research Institute.

[4] Col. 4 = Col. 1 plus Col. 2 plus Col. 3

[5] Col. 5 = Col. 4 in Table 1.

[6] Col. 6 = Col. 4 divided by Col. 5.

malting varieties was multiplied by total barley production. The potential production figures can then be compared with the actual disappearance of Canadian barley used for malting purposes. The almost fourfold increase in potential malting barley production is particularly noteworthy, especially in the context of a not even twofold increase in domestic useage and a not much changed level of malt and malting barley exports.

WORLD TRADE IN BARLEY AND MALTING BARLEY

Barley accounts for approximately 11 percent of the total grain produced on a global basis. The ten largest barley producing countries account for 75 percent of total world output. The U.S.S.R. produces approximately 30 percent and France, Canada, U.K., U.S.A., W. Germany and Spain each produce between 4-7 percent of world barley output.

World trade in barley is highly concentrated, particularly on the export side. The top five exporting countries account for 79 percent of world exports and the top ten exporting countries for 94 percent. Based on average 1978-1980 figures, Canada is the second largest exporter of barley in the world, following slightly behind France. These two countries alone account for almost 50 percent of world barley exports.

On the import side, trade is also relatively concentrated among only a few countries. Based on average 1978-1980 figures, the top five barley importing countries accounted for almost 50 percent of total world imports. These included the U.S.S.R., Japan, Poland, Italy and Belgium/Luxemburg.

MALTING BARLEY

Malting barley, as opposed to feed barley, is used for brewing and distilling purposes. Like total exports of barley, exports of malting barley are highly concentrated. The five largest exporters account for almost 90 percent of total malting barley exports. In recent years, Australia has been the largest malting barley exporter, followed closely by France and Canada. Canada's principal markets for malting barley have been the U.S.A., Columbia, Peru and the U.K.

MALT

Once malting barley is processed (i.e., germinated and dried), it is referred to as malt. The five largest malt exporting countries account for about 70 percent of total exports and the top ten exporters account for about 90 percent. France is the largest exporter of malt, followed by Belgium-Luxemburg, Australia and Canada. Canada's principal malt markets have traditionally been the U.S.A., Japan, the U.K., the Philippines, Venezuela and Jamaica.

On the import side, Japan is by far the largest importer of malt in the world taking approximately 20 percent of total malt traded. The next largest importer is Brazil, followed by the U.S.S.R. and W. Germany. The top five malt importing countries account for about 50 percent of total malt imports.

BEER

About 85 percent of barley malt produced in the world is used to produce beer. The other 15 percent is used in the production of distilled spirits, non-alcoholic beverages and food products. Thus, the world production level of barley malt is primarily a function of the world demand for beer.

The U.S.A. is by far the largest beer producer in the world, followed by W. Germany, the U.S.S.R, the U.K. and Japan. These top five producers account for over 50 percent of total worldwide beer production.

International trade in beer accounts for less than 5 percent of total world production. This is mainly because of the high cost of transporting beer relative to its value and limited storage life.

RESEARCH AND EXPORTS

As malting barley research improves the genetic quality of Canadian malting barley, Canadian exports of malt and malting barley should rise, especially if Canadian quality improvements are made at a faster rate than competing countries. However, the exact size of this effect is not known. At present all the major barley exporters are conducting about the same amount of malting barley research as Canada is.

ORGANIZATION OF THE CANADIAN MALTING BARLEY INDUSTRY

The actors in the Canadian malting barley industry and their activities are summarized in Table 3 and the flow diagram in Figure 2.

In Canada, malting barley is grown by thousands of farmers; however, all farmer must sell all barley used for malting purposes to the Canadian Wheat Board (CWB). The CWB, in addition to being a monopsony buyer of malting barley, is also a monopoly seller of malting barley to domestic and foreign malsters. After buying malting barley from the CWB, domestic malsters process it and sell it as malt to brewers. The brewers process the malt into beer and, in turn, sell any beer destined for domestic use to the provincial liquor boards at government-negotiated prices. In most provinces, these boards are monopoly sellers of beer to domestic consumers. Even in provinces where they are not the only retail sellers of beer, they still retain complete control of the pricing, taxing and regulation of the retail end of the beer sector.

In the last thirty years barley breeders have released new malting barley varieties that have been superior to existing varieties in one or more agronomic attributes (e.g., higher yielding, more lodge and shatter resistant, earlier maturing). In addition, newer varieties have had progressively higher extract percents and faster germination (associated with higher diastatic power). Selection for these quality type improvements has been largely the result of the influence of the BMBRI on barley breeders.[8]

TABLE 3

THE CANADIAN MALT BARLEY INDUSTRY

Actor	Job	Approx. No.	Location
1) Malt barley growers	Grow barley	>20,000	Mainly in black soil zone, especially around Red Deer, Alta.
2) Grain companies	Handle barley	8	All areas
3) Railways	Transport barley	2	All areas
4) Canadian Wheat Board	Monopsony buyer and monopoly seller of malting barley	1	Winnipeg
5) Malsters	Process barley into malt	3 (1 Co. has > 75% of market)	Montreal, Toronto, Winnipeg, Calgary, Biggar, Thunder Bay
6) Brewers	Process malt into beer	3 Cos. have > 95% of market	Most major centres in Canada
7) Provincial Liquor Boards	Provincial monopsony buyer and monopoly seller of beer	One per province	All areas
8) Consumers	Consume beer	> 5,000,000	All areas
9) Universities	Conduct barley research	5	Saskatoon, Winnipeg, Guelph Montreal, Edmonton
10) Agriculture Canada Research Stations	Conduct barley research	7	Winnipeg, Brandon, Ottawa, Charlottetown, Beaverlodge, Lethbridge, Lacombe
11) Other research institutions			
a) CWB Grain Commissioners) Lab)	Conduct barley research	1 1	Winnipeg Winnipeg
b) Brewing & Malting Barley) Research) Institute)		1	Ailsa Craig, Ont.
c) Cieby-Giby) Seeds)			
12) Registered seed growers	Produce and sell new barley varieties	< 500	All areas
13) Livestock farmers	Feed barley to livestock	> 40,000	All areas, especially in southern Alta.

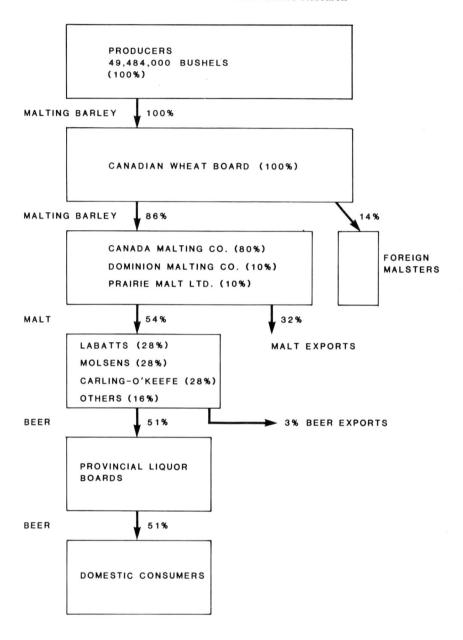

Figure 2

The Main Actors in the Canadian Malting Barley Market[1]

[1] Percentage figures are based on the average of 1979 - 1981 data. They represent the portion of total production going to a particular use or the market share of a firm (boxes are drawn to scale).

These improvements have led to greater productivity and hence to changes in economic surplus in certain subsectors of the barley market. It is the net gain in these surpluses that constitutes the benefits from the investment in malting barley research.

CONCEPTUAL MODEL

Benefits of improved yield and quality attributes of new malting barley varieties can be estimated using the concept of economic surplus. Consider first the effect of higher yielding varieties. With a fixed bundle of other inputs, a new, higher yielding variety allows farmers to produce more output than with an old, lower yielding variety. The net effect is to shift the barley supply curve downward and to the left.

Lindner and Jarrett (1978) have pointed out the importance of determining the manner in which a technological change causes a supply curve to shift. It is postulated that higher yielding barley varieties have led to a divergent shift over time because farmers have more economic incentive to search for and procure new varieties when barley prices are relatively high. This is because their search and procurement costs represent a progressively smaller portion of potential gains from the new variety, as barley prices rise.

Figure 3 illustrates the shift in the malting barley supply curve when the original curve was A_oS_o and the new curve is A_1S_1.

For simplicity, assume linear demand and supply curves. The change in consumers' surplus is given by area $P_o\ M_oM_1P_1$ in Figure 3. The change in producers' surplus is given by area $P_oM_oA_o$ less $P_1M_1A_1$. Rose (1980) suggested that gross annual research benefits could be estimated by:

$$.5*[K*P_o + (A_o-A_1)] + .5*K*P_o(Q_1-Q_o) \tag{1}$$

where the first term represents $A_oM_oBA_1$ and the second term represents area M_oM_1B of Figure 3. Consumers' surplus could be estimated by:

$$Q_a(P_o-P_1) + .5(P_o-P_1)*(Q_1-Q_o) \tag{2}$$

where the first term represents are $P_oM_oBP_1$ and the second term represents area M_oM_1B. Producers' surplus could then be estimated by subtracting consumers surplus from gross annual research benefits.

P_1 and Q_1 are post-adoption price and quantity; P_o and Q_o are pre-adoption price and quantity where:

$$P_o = P_1/[1 - (K*e)/(e+n)] \tag{3}$$

$$Q_o = Q_1/[1 + (K*e*n)/(e+n)]. \tag{4}$$

In these equations, K is the proportionate reduction in average costs of production, measured at Q_o, from adopting the new technology, and e and n are the price elasticity of supply and demand respectively. A_o and A_1 are the pre- and post-adoption intercept terms.[9]

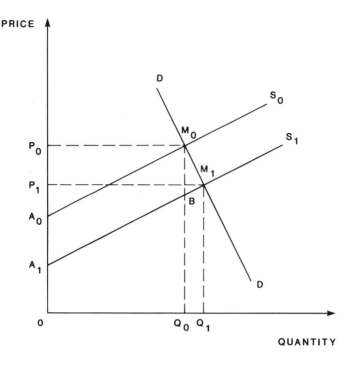

Figure 3
The Effect of Higher Yielding Varieties

Annual estimates of consumers' and producers' surpluses could be made as long as annual values of P_1, Q_1 and K were available and reasonable estimates of e, n and A could be made.

Benefits of the improved quality of malting barley varieties could be calculated in a manner similar to the one just described. As the extract yield increases, brewers can produce a larger quantity of beer from a given quantity of malting barley. Following the work of Mansfield (1977) and others, we will assume that the malsters and brewers[10] face either a flat or upward sloping average cost curve and hence have a flat or upward sloping supply curve for malt and beer.[11] An increase in extract yields would lead to lower average costs and hence produce a downward shift of the beer supply curve from A_0S_0 to A_1S_1. Economic surpluses could be calculated in the previously described manner; however, producers' surplus would become brewers' surplus.

Similarly, the decrease in germination time has reduced the overhead cost of processing each bushel of malting barley by enabling greater output through the same facilities. This causes the malt supply curve to shift downward. Surpluses could once again be calculated; however, calculated producers' surplus would, in this case, refer to malsters' surplus.

A further private benefit may flow to malsters from higher yielding malting barley varieties if they lead to lower malting barley prices to malsters. The lower price of this input would also produce a downward shift in the malt supply curve and create a further increase in the malsters' surplus.

In a perfectly competitive world the generation of the three just-described private surpluses would not be possible. However, in the case of the Canadian brewing and malting industries, such surpluses may be possible, because malting barley prices are negotiated with the CWB and beer prices are negotiated with provincial liquor boards. The ability of the private sector to enjoy these gains in private surplus depends critically on the information, market and bargaining power of private firms vis-à-vis the CWB and the various liquor boards. As long as brewers are able to hide the cost savings associated with the improved quality and quantity of new malting barley varieties, they could continue to enjoy benefits M_1, M_2 and M_3 in Figure 4 (where M_1 is the possible brewers' surplus created by higher extract yields, M_2 is the possible malsters' surplus created by faster germination and M_3 is the possible malsters' surplus created by higher malting barley yields and the implied lower price).

Once these public and private surpluses were calculated, they could be combined with annual research cost estimates to allow the calculation of various rates of return. Building on Hueth, *et al.*'s (1980) definition of internal rates of return for mixed private and public investment, the public rate of return to public investment (r_{ss}) is:

$$\sum_{t=0}^{T} \frac{I_{st}}{(1+r_{ss})^t} = \sum_{t=0}^{T} \frac{C_t + P_t + M_1t + M_2t + M_3t}{(1+r_{ss})^t} \tag{5}$$

and the private rate of return of private investment (r_{pp}) is:

$$\sum_{t=0}^{T} \frac{I_{pt}}{(1+r_{pp})^t} = \sum_{t=0}^{T} \frac{M_{1t} + M_{2t} + M_{3t}}{(1+r_{pp})^t} \tag{6}$$

where t is any year, T is the year in which research ceases to produce benefits, I_s and I_p are public and private investments, and C and P are consumers' and producers' surpluses. M_1, M_2 and M_3 are the private benefits associated with the three possible private surpluses mentioned earlier.

To fully encompass the range of market and bargaining power that might exist between the CWB, malsters/brewers and the liquor boards, this study presents two scenarios which represent two extremes. The true world situation lies somewhere between.

Scenario (1)

The Canadian Wheat Board and liquor boards are fully aware and have sufficient bargaining strength to force private industry to pay for every incremental increase

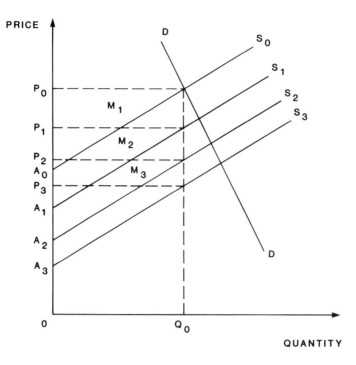

Figure 4
Total Possible Private Surpluses

in quality and/or to reduce malt and beer prices to reflect every decrease in cost so that no increased private surplus is generated.

Scenario (2)

The Canadian Wheat Board and liquor boards are not aware and/or do not have sufficient bargaining strength to force private industry to pay more for better barley quality or to lower beer prices. Hence private industry captures fully surpluses M_1, M_2 and M_3 in Figure 4.

RESEARCH COSTS

The cost of conducting malting barley research in Canada is shared by the private and public sectors. There are three sources of public funds: (1) Agriculture Canada (the largest contributor), (2) universities and associated research institutions and (3) the Canadian Grain Commission.

The private costs (Column 10, Table 4) are expenditures made by the Brewing and Malting Barley Research Institute (BMBRI) in support of malting barley research. The cost includes research grants to universities, Agriculture Canada, in-house research by the Institute and administrative and liaison duties performed

TABLE 4

PRIVATE AND SOCIAL COSTS

Year	(1) Agriculture Canada Man-yrs.	(2) University Researcher Man-yrs.	(3) University Professor Man-yrs.	(4) Other Research Man-yrs.	(5) Graduate Student Man-yrs.	(6) Total Malting Barley Man-yrs. [1]	(7) Estimated Nominal Cost per Man-yr. ('000$)	(8) C.P.I.	(9) Public Cost '000 (1971 $)	(10) Private Cost '000 (1971 $)	(11) Public & Private Cost '000 (1971 $)
51	9.9	.5	2.1	2.0	7.3	10.9	13.3	.709	203.2	80.3	283.5
52	9.9	.5	1.7	2.0	10.4	10.6	14.4	.718	211.7	80.2	291.9
53	10.1	.5	1.7	2.0	1.9	10.7	15.0	.714	226.0	86.4	312.4
54	10.1	1.9	2.2	2.0	2.5	12.2	16.6	.720	280.5	78.2	358.7
55	9.8	2.0	2.2	2.0	4.9	12.0	17.1	.721	283.5	76.2	359.7
56	9.8	2.0	2.4	2.0	6.3	12.0	18.0	.729	299.2	73.2	372.4
57	9.8	2.0	2.4	2.0	3.1	12.0	18.9	.748	308.1	121.6	429.7
58	10.3	2.0	2.6	2.0	8.5	12.7	21.0	.766	348.8	198.2	547.0
59	15.0	2.0	2.7	2.0	3.2	16.3	21.6	.773	455.1	86.6	541.7
60	14.3	1.5	2.9	2.0	4.9	15.5	22.9	.782	453.7	91.4	545.1
61	14.4	1.8	3.0	2.0	3.9	15.8	23.6	.790	473.6	96.8	570.4
62	14.3	1.8	3.0	2.0	5.3	15.8	24.5	.800	482.8	90.6	573.4
63	14.3	1.8	3.5	1.0	3.0	15.5	25.7	.807	494.7	127.4	622.1
64	14.4	1.8	3.5	3.0	8.0	15.5	28.7	.815	547.0	128.7	675.7
65	14.9	1.8	3.0	3.0	3.1	17.0	32.3	.830	660.2	95.5	755.7
66	15.6	1.5	4.1	3.0	7.0	18.2	35.2	.856	746.3	106.1	852.4
67	15.4	2.1	3.9	2.0	5.0	17.5	36.7	.885	724.5	104.0	828.5
68	16.6	2.3	4.0	3.0	6.6	19.4	39.2	.922	826.4	112.1	938.5
69	16.4	3.1	4.7	3.0	6.1	20.4	42.3	.958	899.7	107.4	1,007.1
70	16.0	3.1	4.9	3.0	8.9	20.3	47.5	.985	977.8	113.2	1,091.0
71	16.2	4.9	4.9	3.0	5.8	21.8	50.6	1.000	1,098.2	112.0	1,210.2
72	16.5	5.1	4.9	3.0	4.9	22.1	57.1	1.039	1,217.4	115.0	1,332.4
73	17.9	5.2	4.9	3.0	10.2	23.3	61.3	1.103	1,291.8	107.2	1,399.0
74	18.8	5.3	4.8	2.5	4.3	23.6	65.7	1.217	1,270.6	105.9	1,376.5
75	19.0	5.2	5.4	2.0	6.2	23.7	73.6	1.354	1,287.0	118.2	1,405.2
76	20.0	7.6	5.2	2.0	5.8	26.1	78.7	1.470	1,400.5	93.1	1,493.6
77	20.0	7.0	5.2	2.0	9.8	25.7	84.7	1.595	1,362.9	95.1	1,458.0
78	19.6	6.9	5.7	2.0	9.2	25.7	91.3	1.730	1,352.4	94.6	1,447.0
79	17.6	7.4	5.2	2.0	7.3	24.9	99.0	1.885	1,320.8	89.2	1,410.0
80	17.9	6.0	5.2	3.0	4.1	24.1	108.0	2.077	1,246.9	82.2	1,329.1
81	17.8	6.1	5.1	3.0	7.6	24.0	118.3	2.328	1,221.0	87.6	1,308.6

[1] Assume 75% of all barley research concerns itself with malting varieties.

by Institute personnel. It should be noted that the private sector contribution has been declining as a percentage of total research expenditures on malting barley since 1951.

The public sector costs were estimated from person-year research efforts of Agriculture Canada, universities and the Canadian Grain Commission. Within each research organization, the number of person-years of research was collected and multiplied by the nominal cost of a person-year of research. The largest share of public sector barley research was done by Agriculture Canada (Table 4, Column 1). The nominal cost of doing research as developed by Zentner (Table 4, Column 7) for Agriculture Canada was used to estimate the monetary cost of doing barley research at all public institutions. The number of graduate students involved in malting barley research is reported in Table 4, Column 5; however, it is not included in the aggregate total social costs.

RESEARCH RETURNS

Research benefits often do not occur in the same year as the expenditures occur. Evenson has estimated a lag of about seven years between the time the expenditure is made and the benefits are realized. Zentner used a seven- to eight-year lag for wheat research in Canada. Once research and development expenditures stop, benefits will continue to flow, assuming some form of maintenance research. The benefits from malting barley research are shown in Table 5, assuming a seven-year lag and 30 percent maintenance cost to maintain the research benefits for seven years into the future.

The maximum possible private benefits from faster germination (i.e., building cost reductions) were calculated by taking the product of capital cost per bushel, bushels processed, building cost index and percentage decrease in time required to produce malt. The maximum possible private benefits from higher extract yields were calculated by taking the product of malting barley price, bushels processed and percentage decrease in bushels needed. The maximum possible private benefits from higher yields (and the resulting lower malting barley price) were calculated by taking the product of bushels processed and the predicted difference in price caused by higher yields. The results of these calculations appear in Table 5.

The estimated rates of return to the private and public sector investment in malting barley research are given in Table 6. Under Scenario (1) the public sector returns 50 percent on public funds and 74 percent on private funds. Under Scenario (2) the public sector also returns 50 percent on public funds and 74 percent on private funds. The private sector returns 16 percent on public funds and 33 percent on private investment.[12] These rates of return are well within the range of those reported in previous agricultural and manufacturing rate of return studies. They indicate that the public sector has had a very high rate of return on private funds even though the private investment is small. This suggests that joint agricultural research can greatly benefit investors from both sectors.

TABLE 5

ESTIMATED ANNUAL RETURNS TO BREEDING EFFORT ('000,000 1971 $)

Year	Feed Sector[1]		Malt Sector[1]			Possible Private Benefits[1]			
	Consumer Surplus	Producer Surplus	Consumer Surplus	Producer Surplus	Total Public Surplus	Building Cost Saving	Reduction in Quantity Required	Reduction in Barley Price	Total Possible Private Benefit
1951	0	0	0	0	0	0	0	0	0
1952	0	0	0	0	0	0	0	0	0
1953	0	0	0	0	0	0	0	0	0
1954	0	0	0	0	0	0	0	0	0
1955	0	0	0	0	0	0	0	0	0
1956	0	0	0	0	0	0	0	0	0
1957	0	0	0	0	0	0	0	0	0
1958	.19	1.74	.99	.20	3.12	.01	.02	.36	.39
1959	.27	2.44	.92	.20	3.83	.02	.05	.41	.48
1960	.22	2.05	.98	.20	3.46	.03	.07	.42	.53
1961	.24	2.18	.98	.21	3.61	.04	.08	.48	.60
1962	.13	1.23	1.02	.24	2.62	.06	.10	.58	.74
1963	.23	2.14	.73	.17	3.28	.07	.09	.52	.67
1964	.33	3.03	1.03	.24	4.63	.08	.09	.59	.77
1965	.24	2.23	1.16	.27	3.90	.10	.10	.72	.91
1966	.40	3.71	1.12	.25	5.50	.11	.17	.80	1.09
1967	.68	6.24	1.30	.30	8.53	.13	.24	.87	1.24
1968	.49	4.50	1.11	.23	6.33	.14	.27	.81	1.22
1969	.59	5.42	1.14	.24	7.40	.17	.30	.76	1.23
1970	.47	4.27	1.19	.21	6.15	.20	.35	.68	1.23
1971	.58	5.31	1.51	.28	7.68	.26	.40	.81	1.47
1972	.85	7.80	1.52	.27	10.45	.31	.41	.89	1.61
1973	1.29	11.83	3.16	.52	16.88	.34	.76	1.81	2.92
1974	2.17	19.89	4.10	.96	27.14	.37	1.03	2.50	3.89
1975	1.54	14.41	4.72	.89	21.31	.41	1.03	2.67	4.12
1976	1.76	16.18	3.78	.84	22.59	.41	.93	2.19	3.53
1977	1.58	14.56	2.84	.61	19.61	.47	.85	1.79	3.12
1978	1.48	13.61	2.60	.57	18.36	.55	.75	1.47	2.76
1979	1.29	11.91	3.06	.56	16.85	.63	1.00	1.87	3.50
1980	1.32	12.20	3.32	.71	18.09	.68	1.31	2.39	4.38
1981	2.22	20.52	3.41	.76	26.93	.71	1.26	2.34	4.31
1982-88p	1.61	14.58	3.43	.68	20.52	.67	1.19	2.20	4.06

[1] Based on elasticity of malt supply = elasticity of feed supply = .7, elasticity of malt demand = -.51, elasticity of feed demand = -10.0, price axis intercept = .3 of annual feed barley price.

p Projected annual benefit is the average annual real benefit 1979-1981.

TABLE 6

ESTIMATED PRIVATE AND PUBLIC RATES OF RETURN
(in Percents)

	Internal Rate of Return[1]	External Rate of Return[1]	Internal Rate of Return[2]	External Rate of Return[2]
r_{ss}	50	1,357	51	1,370
r_{sp}	74	8,393	74	8,476
r_{ps}	16	206	17	218
r_{pp}	33	1,272	35	1,347

[1] Scenario (2) with the same assumptions as Table 5.

[2] Scenario (2) with the same assumptions as Table 5 except that elasticity of demand for feed and malt is reduced by 20 percent. In this case, producer surplus in the malt sector is actually reduced with new varieties. However, because the producer surplus in the feed sector is so large, social rates of return would not change greatly even if malt demand had an elasticity of, say, -.05.

The external rates of return (i.e., benefit-cost ratios) were large in all cases reported in Table 6. It appears from these results that the public sector has underinvested in malting barley research (mainly because of the extra feed that was produced). This result is consistent with most other studies of agricultural rates of return.

The sensitivity of the results to a change in the elasticity of malt demand was small with private returns increasing slightly and producer returns declining (shown in Table 6). When the length of future benefits was increased from seven to twenty years, the internal rates of return did not change; however, the external rates increased, as would be expected. When the intercept on the supply curve was changed to $A_1 = .5P$, the rates were 85-90 percent of those reported in Table 6. The size of benefits appeared to be most sensitive to the calculated shift in the production function. However, it is doubtful that the estimated annual K-values that were used were much in error since the experimental data was well documented and extensive. In summary, the results are robust within any range of reasonable parameters.

MARGINAL RETURNS

The preceding portion of this paper indicated the average rates of return that have been enjoyed over the thirty-year period from 1951 to 1981. However, those people presently making research investment allocations should, perhaps, be more interested in the expected marginal rate of return. With this in mind, an attempt was made to estimate the marginal rates of return to malting barley research.

To do this, one must think of research as an input into the production of economic surpluses. In the case of malting barley, it was postulated that the annual real economic surplus generated from malting barley varieties was mainly a function of annual real barley prices, annual acreage planted to malting varieties and the annual amount of total (i.e., private plus public) funds spent on malting barley research seven years previously. When these variables were regressed against total real public surplus (i.e., producer plus consumer surplus) in a linear equation, 98 percent of the variation in total real public surplus was explained.[13] In addition, no serial correlation was indicated. To facilitate the calculation of the marginal product of the research variable, a regression similar to the one just described was run; however, all the observations were expressed as natural logarithms. This resulted in the following:

$$\ln B = -14.21 + .9712 \ln TC + 1.0700 \ln AC + .7869 \ln P \qquad (7)$$

$$(-9.63) \quad (14.39) \qquad (9.03) \qquad (7.77)$$

$$R^{-2} = .98 \qquad N = 24 \qquad D.W. = 2.01$$

where B is total surplus, TC is total research investment lagged seven years, AC is acres planted to malting barley varieties and P is average barley price (note: t-statistics are in parentheses).

The marginal product of the research variable was calculated at the minimum, mean and maximum levels of investment that occurred in years 1951-1974 using the following formula for the first derivative of B with respect to TC, and holding the value of AC and P constant at their means:

$$\frac{dB}{dTc} = \frac{.9712*B}{TC} \qquad (8)$$

The results showed the following:

when TC was 283,553 MP_{TC} = 14.069
       TC was 719,812 MP_{TC} = 13.696
       TC was 1,398,970 MP_{TC} = 13.434

or graphically (Figure 5).

These results indicate that the marginal product of research (MP2T2C) declined as the level of research expenditures increased. However, even at the highest level of research funding, over thirteen dollars of public benefits were produced from every one dollar of research investment. This is very high and would seem to indicate that barley research expenditures could be increased severalfold without greatly altering the high public rates of return that have been enjoyed previously.

When this same procedure was tried with private investment and private benefits, serial correlation was detected. Once this was corrected, private benefits appeared to be only significantly related to barley prices and to be statistically unrelated to private research expenditures or barley acreage. This seems logical on several accounts. First, private benefits have been fluctuating but generally rising. The annual fluctuations have been almost totally due to annual changes in

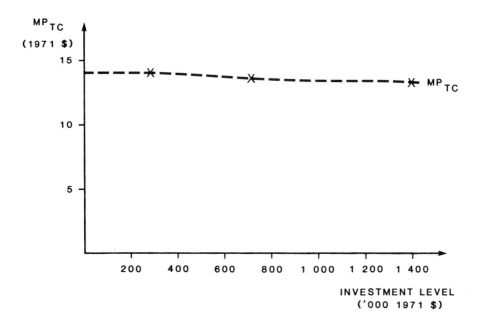

Figure 5

The Marginal Product (MP$_{TC}$) of Malting Barley Research Investment

barley prices. Hence barley prices should be significantly related. Second, malsters and brewers buy approximately the same amount of malting barley each year; hence barley acreage may have little effect on private benefits. Third, private investment in barley research has declined in real terms over the years. In the early 1950s, it represented over 30 percent of all malting barley research investment; it now represents less than 8 percent. Since private benefits are the product of combined public and private investment in research, it seems logical that private benefits, especially in recent years, would not be affected in a significant way by private research expenditures.

Thus, the problem of how to estimate the marginal product of private investment still remained. An alternative approach would be to take the estimated marginal product curve for total research expenditures and substitute in present real research investment (e.g., 1981 total real investment was $1,308,600; the marginal product of an additional dollar at this level of investment would be about $13.45). In recent years total possible private benefits have averaged about 20 percent of total public surplus. This would imply that an extra dollar put in by private industry would produce, after seven years, about $13.45[14] in public benefits and $2.69 in private benefits. From a private point of view, a possible return of $2.69 (in real dollars) after seven years converts to a real internal rate of return of about 15 percent. (The corresponding real public internal rate of return is about 45 percent.) This private rate of return is probably not that much different from returns that can be earned from other successful private investments.

If private industry can convince the public sector to make a greater real investment in malting barley research, private industry will still enjoy the additional private benefits while incurring only the additional cost of an intensified lobbying effort. Almost certainly, the private rate of return would be greater if the intensified lobbying method was chosen over additional direct private research expenditures.

The expected public rate of return is so high that it should encourage more real public expenditure in the area of barley research. However, as noted before, most of the public gains have been in the form of producer surpluses in the feed sector due to higher yields. This implies that the public sector could enjoy an even higher rate of return if it would concentrate strictly on developing higher yielding feed barley varieties.

However, the existence of grants and liaison work from the private sector is likely to keep public sector research institutions on a barley research path that concentrates on both quantity and quality improvements. From a private point of view, this is likely one of the most superior research strategies that could be chosen since privately desired research is being done at close to minimal private cost. The private objectives now probably should be to encourage more public investment while keeping private investment just above the level necessary to effectively induce work on malting barley quality improvements at public research institutions. Such a private strategy is presently adding about 8 percent to the total research budget but costs the public sector the difference between the public surpluses that would be generated if only feed barley research were conducted and the public surpluses that would be generated under the present orientation.

In conclusion, it appears that Canadian malsters and brewers picked, by accident or by skill, a very successful investment R&D malting barley research strategy. Initially they invested relatively heavily to get public research institutions to consider quality improvements in addition to the traditional quantity improvements. This generated a very high marginal product to each private investment dollar by getting public funds committed to a previously private objective. Once public funds and resources were committed, the marginal product of additional private investment declined to the point where it became competitive with other private investments. Once this point was reached, there was, and still is, little economic incentive in increasing real annual private R&D expenditures as long as public sector investment is so large, relative to the private sector. However, this situation would change dramatically if the public sector decided to stop trying to improve quality traits (i.e., if they concentrated entirely on feed barley improvements).

DISCUSSION AND SCOPE FOR FURTHER RESEARCH

The public rate of return to public investment in the development of better malting barley varieties has been high relative to many private and public investments. This is consistent with the findings of other studies on the public rates of return to agricultural research (e.g., Nagy and Furtan; Zentner). A private rate of return of less than 33 percent is also consistent with the private rates estimated by Mansfield, *et al.* This study, based mainly on Ulrich (1983), documents a Canadian case situation where public and private sectors combined forces to conduct research. The benefits that each sector enjoyed were enhanced by the research expenditures made by the other sector. These results should encourage more joint research efforts in the future.

However, many questions remain. For instance, what is an equitable means of increasing public R&D expenditures in Canada? What effect is research likely to have on the structure, conduct and performance of agri-industries if these industries induce public institutions to do research that has definite private benefits? From a private point of view, what research strategy is likely to produce the highest rates of return?

In answer to the last question, the author hypothesizes that, from a private point of view, long-run private returns to research would be maximized by giving relatively large grants to public institutions for a time period sufficiently long that the public institutions permanently commit funds, facilities and staff to a research field of interest to the private firm. Once this permanent commitment is achieved, the private firm gradually reduces, in real terms, their funding effort in this area[15] so they have more funds to grant to additional public institutions doing research in another field of private interest. When these additional institutions permanently commit resources to this other field of private interest, the private firms once again reduce their funding so that another round of public-private joint research in another area can be started.

In the case of malting barley, a look at the yearly change in the benefit/cost ratios shows that, although the public ratio has not changed much over the years, the private ratio has gotten progressively higher as the absolute size of private benefits increased and the portion of total malting barley research funded by the private sector decreased. Such a private strategy might maximize private returns to research but will it maximize public welfare as well? What would the public rate of return have been if barley breeders had devoted all their efforts to increasing feed barley yields instead of devoting some of their efforts to increasing malting barley quality? Answers to these types of questions need to be increasingly found as public research institutions seek increased private funding to make up the shortage of research funds caused by government budgetary cutbacks.

NOTES

1. A good review of the literature on this topic is provided in Minnesota Agricultural Experiment Station, *Evaluation of Agricultural Research*, University of Minnesota, Miscellaneous Publication 8-1981.

2. For instance, see studies by Griliches (1975), Mansfield (1968 and 1977), Minasian (1969) or Terleckyj (1974).

3. Although it is not always the case, the social rate of return is approximately twice the private rate of return.

4. These firms are usually in subsectors that enable new discoveries to be patented or sold (e.g., farm machinery, hybrid seed).

5. For instance, a firm may give a grant to a university department providing specified research is carried out. The university, in turn, may not charge the firm the full cost of doing the research because its buildings, equipment and staff are a "sunk cost."

6. A weighted yield index of all barley varieties shows a less than 8 percent yield increase due to higher yielding varieties between 1951 and 1981. This is included in the yield per acre figures.

7. In the early 1950s, about 31 percent of this potential production was actually used for malting; in the late 1970s, it was down to 14 percent.

8. A question then arises, if breeders had not spent some of their efforts developing better quality varieties, could they have developed varieties that were even higher yielding than present varieties? Was the gain in quality worth the loss in potential yield improvement?

9. Lindner and Jarrett (1978) point out that a positive intercept is more appealing than a zero intercept. They also argue that, although the value of these intercepts can only be approximated, the level of estimated research benefits is relatively insensitive to the value of A used.

10. Because two Canadian brewers own a controlling interest in the major malting company, the potential benefits private firms receive will not be separated into malster benefits and brewer benefits.

11. It can be shown that the surpluses previously described would be of the same approximate magnitude if the supply curve is flat or upward sloping.

12. It was noted earlier that the actual private rates of return are somewhere between zero and those estimated under Scenario (2) depending on the private marketing and bargaining power that actually existed.

13. When the only explanatory variable was the seven-year lagged research term, 73 percent of the deviation in total public surplus was explained; however, serial correlation was present.

14. If barley acreage and/or real barley prices were higher, in seven years time these returns would be higher since quantity improvements would be spread over more production and/or higher valued production.

15. Although short-term private returns would rise with a sudden withdrawal of all private funds, the long-term negative public relations that could be generated from such action would probably more than off-set the value of such a short-term gain.

REFERENCES

Currie, J.M., J.A. Murphy, and A. Schmitz. "The Concept of Economic Surplus and Its Use in Economic Analysis." *Economic Journal* 81 (1971): 741-799.

Gibney, S.L., and W.H. Furtan. "Welfare Effects of New Crop Variety Licensing Regulations: The Case of Canadian Malt Barley." *American Journal of Agricultural Economics* 65 (1983): 142-147.

Griliches, Z. "Returns to Research and Development Expenditures in the Private Sector." Conference on Research in Income and Wealth, 1975.

Hueth, D., A. Schmitz, and R. Cooper. "Rates of Return from Investment in Research." Paper presented to the Lawrence Livermore Laboratory, October 1980. (Mimeographed.)

Laforge, Arthur J. "A Regional Econometric Model of the Canadian Feed Sector." M.Sc. thesis, University of Saskatchewan, 1973.

Lindner, R.K., and F.G. Jarrett. "Supply Shifts and the Size of Research Benefits." *American Journal of Agricultural Economics* 60 (1978): 48-56.

Mansfield, E. *Industrial Research and Technological Innovation.* New York: W.W. Norton for the Cowles Foundation for Research in Economics at Yale University, 1968.

Mansfield, E., J. Rapoport, A. Romeo, E. Villani, S. Wagner, and F. Husic. *The Production and Application of New Industrial Technology.* New York: W.W. Norton, 1977.

Minasian, J. "Research and Development, Production Functions and Rates of Return." *American Economic Review*, May 1969.

Norton, G.W., W.L. Fishel, A.A. Paulsen, and W.B. Sundquist. *Evaluation of Agricultural Research.* Minneapolis: University of Minnesota, Minnesota Agricultural Experiment Station Miscellaneous Publication No. 8, 1981.

Rose, F. "Supply Shifts and Research Benefits: Comment." *American Journal of Agricultural Economics* 62 (November 1980): 834-837.

Ruttan, Vernon W. *Agricultural Research Policy.* Minneapolis: University of Minnesota Press, 1982.

Ryan, T.J. *The Demand for Barley for Food and Beverage Uses in Australia.* Dept. of Agriculture, Government of Victoria, Research Series No. 115, 1981.

Spriggs, J. *An Econometric Analysis of Canadian Grains and Oilseeds.* U.S.D.A. ERD Technical Bulletin No. 1662, 1981.

Terleckyj, N. *Effects of R and D on the Productivity Growth of Industries: An Exploratory Study.* National Planning Association, 1974.

Ulrich, Alvin. "Beer and Malting Barley: A Case of Jointly Funded Public and Private Research." M.Sc. thesis, University of Saskatchewan, 1983.

Zentner, Robert. "An Economic Evaluation of Public Wheat Research Expenditures in Canada." Ph.D. diss., University of Minnesota, 1981.

CHAPTER 10

RETURNS TO PUBLIC INVESTMENT IN CANADIAN WHEAT AND RAPESEED RESEARCH

R. P. Zentner

INTRODUCTION

Investment in agricultural research is made with the expectation that the present value of the future benefits derived from the research activity will exceed the opportunity costs of their generation. In Canada, approximately 90 percent of the total investment in agricultural research is supported by general revenue or public taxation (McLaughlin, 1977). This widespread commitment of public funds to agricultural research is considered necessary for two reasons. The first is related to the structure of the industry. Private farm-firms do not generally undertake agricultural research activities because they are too atomistic and lack the necessary technical abilities, skills and resource base to support the level of investment and risk associated with conducting research. The second reason for public investment in agricultural research is related to the nature of the research output itself. For many types of agricultural research, the output (i.e., new knowledge) cannot be embodied in some physical input or intermediate product, but becomes freely available to everyone once it is produced. Markets do not exist and prices are not established for the research output. Consequently, private non-farm firms lack adequate profit incentives to undertake this type of research. [1]

Over the past several decades, doubts have arisen regarding the social value of these public research investments and the efficiency with which the scarce resources are being allocated among the full array of investment opportunities. Canadian agricultural research scientists and administrators are being held accountable for the resources being utilized and for the impacts on society from the technologies and information (or lack of it) that are generated. This, in turn, has created the need for more and better information on the nature, extent and distribution of the social costs and social benefits from public agricultural research activities.

This paper examines the empirical evidence on whether public investment in Canadian wheat and rapeseed research has constituted socially profitable use of scarce public resources, and to what extent the social benefits from these research activities accrued to producers and non-producers (i.e., consumers) respectively. Only the ''first round'' or direct effects are considered. Secondary effects, such as the impact on input supply industries, processing and marketing industries, and on other sectors of the economy are largely ignored. The discussion draws primarily on the work by Zentner (1982) for wheat and that of Nagy and Furtan (1978) for rapeseed. The study by Zentner (1982) dealt with Canadian wheat research activities conducted over the period 1946-1979. Wheat was defined to include hard red spring, durum and winter wheats. Two research scenarios were examined. The first included research activities related exclusively to the development of genetically superior varieties of wheat. The second included all research activities relevant to the production of wheat. The study by Nagy and Furtan (1978) dealt with the Canadian rapeseed breeding program and considered the period 1960-61 to 1974-75.

THEORETICAL AND METHODOLOGICAL CONSIDERATIONS

THE MEASUREMENT OF SOCIAL COSTS

The question of what should be counted as social costs is a troublesome issue for many economists. The usual answer is that it should include the opportunity costs of the resources being utilized in the research discovery and extension processes. It is frequently assumed that the opportunity cost of a resource is reflected by its market price. When this is true, the resulting sum of opportunity costs will provide an accurate measure of the social costs of conducting research and distributing the new knowledge. However, if externalities are present and are not appropriately accounted for, the market price underestimates the full opportunity cost of a resource (Kaldor, 1971).

In the studies by Zentner (1982) and by Nagy and Furtan (1978), only direct resource expenditures were considered as social costs. Estimates of public expenditures on wheat and rapeseed research were made from information on person-years obtained from annual listings of professional personnel at the various research institutions. Wheat breeding was defined to include only those activities related to the development of new wheat varieties, wheat genetics and wheat variety assessment. A similar definition was used for rapeseed breeding research. The estimates for the all-wheat research scenarios included not only the person-years attributable solely to wheat (e.g., wheat fertility or development of wheat stem sawfly resistant varieties), but also portions of person-years devoted to lines of research activity applicable to all crops or to particular groups of crops (e.g., soils, weeds, insects). The weights used in apportioning these latter person-years were the ratio of the wheat area to the total area in the particular crop groupings.

The person-years were converted into monetary values by multiplying by the annual cost of supporting a professional scientist.[2] The monetary values for the wheat research scenarios were deflated to 1971 dollars by an index of associate professors' salaries, while those for rapeseed breeding research were deflated to 1961 dollars by the Consumer Price Index (Table 1).[3]

Annual estimates of wheat variety and all wheat extension expenditures were also made (Table 1). These estimates were derived from the public accounts of the relevant departments in universities, provincial governments and the Federal Government. Because of the lack of adequate categorization in the financial records, an apportioning procedure was used. It was based on two assumptions. The first was that the proportion of the total agricultural extension expenditures applicable to the production of wheat was in direct relation to the importance of the crop. A five-year moving average ratio of wheat sales to total farm income was used. The second was that the proportion of the total wheat extension expenditures applicable to the dissemination of information on new wheat varieties was in direct relation to the ratio of expenditures on wheat breeding research relative to total wheat research. The resulting wheat extension expenditures were deflated to 1971 dollars by an index of associate professors' salaries.

TABLE 1

ESTIMATED PUBLIC EXPENDITURES ON WHEAT RESEARCH AND EXTENSION AND ON RAPESEED BREEDING RESEARCH ACTIVITIES IN CANADA

Year	Wheat Breeding Research	All Wheat Research	Wheat Variety Extension	All Wheat Extension	Rapeseed Breeding Research
	--------(Thousands of 1971 dollars)--------				(Thousands of 1961 dollars)
1946	666.9	3092.0	265.3	1230.1	
1947	754.9	3513.5	372.3	1732.8	
1948	979.7	4646.6	430.3	2040.9	
1949	1060.0	5057.2	460.9	2198.9	
1950	1099.4	5467.8	455.4	2213.6	
1951	1107.6	5505.3	460.3	2287.9	
1952	1160.5	5939.3	485.6	2485.3	
1953	1154.2	5751.3	520.0	2590.9	
1954	1223.1	6060.8	516.1	2557.4	
1955	1211.6	6160.0	506.2	2573.8	
1956	1277.3	5954.3	472.8	2536.2	
1957	1215.8	6059.3	473.8	2361.4	
1958	1170.7	5877.8	434.4	2180.9	
1959	1106.1	5551.4	425.6	2136.2	
1960	1102.7	5513.2	441.2	2206.1	23.2
1961	1120.4	5563.6	452.4	2246.7	48.7
1962	1106.5	5872.8	452.2	2400.3	81.2
1963	1123.7	5887.5	504.9	2645.3	106.3
1964	1175.8	6433.7	520.5	2847.9	157.2
1965	1220.6	6975.9	503.7	2878.6	241.3
1966	1240.1	7285.5	515.9	3031.1	368.0
1967	1187.8	7175.3	532.3	3216.4	514.6
1968	1235.4	7932.0	519.0	3332.0	666.4
1969	1325.9	7627.5	520.4	2993.8	900.0
1970	1321.5	7819.1	526.6	3115.9	1179.5
1971	1311.0	8025.7	583.3	3080.2	1458.7
1972	1391.1	8394.4	569.4	3436.2	1796.0
1973	1360.5	8326.2	632.9	3873.1	2122.2
1974	1338.6	8143.6	793.2	4825.3	2558.8
1975	1329.0	8352.6	864.3	5432.0	
1976	1371.9	9129.7	843.6	5613.7	
1977	1363.0	9333.4	837.1	5732.5	
1978	1347.1	9137.9	838.1	5685.2	
1979	1369.6	9247.0	843.5	5694.8	

Extension expenditures related to the dissemination of information on new rapeseed varieties were not calculated and, thus, not included as social costs. Neither study made allowances for labour "displacement" resulting from the development of new wheat or rapeseed technologies. Zentner (1982) argued that the inclusion of such allowances was inappropriate for two reasons. First, it is unclear whether the labour leaving agriculture was in fact "displaced" by new technologies or simply "attracted out" of agriculture by better opportunities (Kislev and Peterson, 1981). Furthermore, few data exist as to whether the labour leaving agriculture was able to find alternative employment. Second, the majority of the new technologies developed by public research activities tend not to be highly labour saving.

THE MEASUREMENT OF SOCIAL BENEFITS

The theoretical framework used in both studies for measuring the magnitude and distribution of the social benefits (or losses) from the research activities was similar to that outlined by Hayami and Akino (1977). It involved the use of the Marshallian concept of economic surplus as a measure of social welfare. Economic surplus is composed of two components — consumers' surplus and producers' surplus. Consumers' surplus is defined as the difference between the amount of income required to just compensate consumers for the loss of a given quantity of product, and that which consumers actually pay to obtain the product. It is represented by the area below the ordinary demand curve and above the equilibrium price line.[4] Producers' surplus (or economic rent) is defined with respect to the product supply curve. It is the difference between the total revenue required to just compensate suppliers for supplying a given quantity of final product, and that which is actually received from the sale of the product. Producers' surplus is represented by the area above the supply curve and below the equilibrium price line.

The returns or social benefits from agricultural research are measured in terms of changes in consumers' and producers' surpluses. The changes are brought about by the upward shift in the aggregate production function resulting from the adoption of the new technologies developed by research. The upward shift in the production function (or alternatively, the increased productivity) lowers the marginal costs of production which, in turn, causes the aggregate supply curve for the product to shift outward. When this occurs additional consumers' surplus is created since larger quantities of the product are made available at lower prices. At the same time, additional producers' surplus may also be created from the reduction in production costs and increased quantities of product marketed. The combined effects of the change in consumers' and producers' surpluses represent the total social benefit from the research effort.

To illustrate the theoretical framework, consider the following diagram (Figure 1). The total derived demand curve for the product of interest is given by the curve DD^1. The curve S_N represents the supply of product that exists under the current state of technology. At market equilibrium, price and quantity are given by P_N and Q_N respectively. Consumers' surplus is given by the area P_NBD and producers' surplus is given by the area P_NBO.

The curve S_O represents the supply of the product that would have existed had there been no research undertaken to develop new technologies. It reflects the increased marginal costs of production if the new technologies were to suddenly

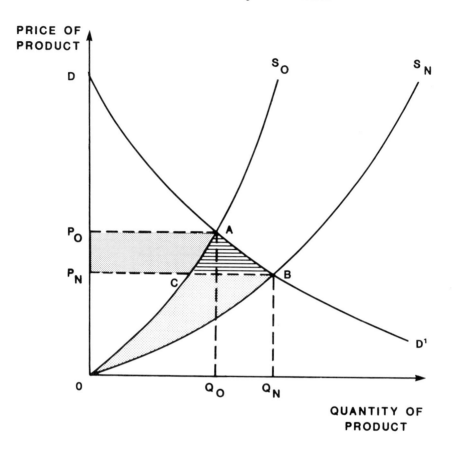

Figure 1

A Theoretical Model for Measuring the Social Benefits of Research

disappear and be replaced by the old technologies. At market equilibrium, price and quantity would be P_O and Q_O respectively. Consumers' surplus is given by the area P_OAD, while producers' surplus is represented by the area P_OAO.

The social benefits attributable to the research activities are obtained by aggregating the changes in consumers' and producers' surpluses. The change in consumers' surplus is given by the area ABC + area P_NP_OAC. This represents a gain to consumers as a result of the drop in the price of the product $(P_O - P_N)$ and the increased quantity made available $(Q_N - Q_O)$. The change in producers' surplus is given by the area CBO - area P_NP_OAC. This represents a possible gain to producers because of the lower costs of production, increased quantity marketed, but reduced product price. Whether producers actually gain or lose is related to the elasticities of the supply and demand curves and can only be determined empirically. The total social benefit or net gain to society from the research activities is represented by the area ABC + area CBO.[5]

To implement this theoretical framework, annual information on several aspects is required. This includes the price elasticities (or price responsiveness) of the relevant supply and demand curves, the equilibrium prices and quantities of the product under the new level of technology, and the rate of shift in the aggregate production function (or alternatively, the aggregate supply function) that is attributable to the research activities.[6] The price elasticity of the Canadian wheat supply curve (i.e., 1.2364) was empirically estimated and was considered to have been constant throughout the period of study, whereas the price elasticity of the Canadian wheat demand curve (i.e., -2.35 to -7.11) was computed annually by weighting the elasticities of the domestic and foreign components by their relative importance. In the case of rapeseed, both the price elasticity of supply (i.e., 1.96) and of demand (i.e., -.285) were empirically estimated and assumed to have been constant throughout the study period. The annual equilibrium prices and quantities for wheat and rapeseed were taken from published records.

Aggregate Production Function Shifts Attributable to Canadian Wheat and Rapeseed Breeding Research

The annual shifts in the aggregate wheat and rapeseed production functions attributable to Canadian wheat and rapeseed breeding research activities were obtained by calculating the weighted average yield increases of the new varieties relative to chosen base varieties assuming the same level of input usage (Table 2). The weights used were the proportions of the total wheat or rapeseed area planted to the new varieties.[7]

Data from the "Cooperative Wheat Variety Trials" and the "Cooperative Rapeseed Variety Trials" conducted under the auspices of the Expert Committee on Grain Breeding, Grain Diseases and Grain Quality were used in computing the varietal contributions. The weights or variety proportions were taken from the "Annual Crop Variety Survey" conducted by the Cooperative Producers Limited and, previous to 1972, by the Searle Grain Company and Line Elevator Farm Service.

Several aspects about the estimation procedure, data source and assumptions deserve comment. The first relates to the use of experimental data. It is well recognized that experimental yields overestimate farm level yields. However, several factors tend to reduce the level of "experimental bias" in these studies. First, only percentage changes in yields and not absolute yield levels were used. It may not be unreasonable to expect that the same proportional changes in yield apply at the farm level. Second, the application of fertilizers, herbicides and insecticides used in the Cooperative Tests were generally set at recommended levels and not output maximizing levels. Third, the Cooperative Tests were conducted over a significant number of locations within each region and the average results used in the studies.

TABLE 2

**ANNUAL ESTIMATES OF THE SHIFT (%) IN THE AGGREGATE WHEAT
AND RAPESEED PRODUCTION FUNCTIONS ATTRIBUTABLE
TO PUBLIC RESEARCH[1]**

Year	Wheat Breeding Research	Rapeseed Breeding Research	All Wheat[2] Research
1956	2.22		3.13
1957	3.00		5.82
1958	2.86		6.05
1959	2.60		8.48
1960	0.21		7.46
1961	0.32		9.10
1962	0.84		9.59
1963	0.93		8.55
1964	0.92	0.6	9.09
1965	0.82	1.4	8.15
1966	1.08	3.6	6.32
1967	2.31	5.1	6.09
1968	3.19	5.9	6.39
1969	3.88	8.8	8.12
1970	3.32	9.6	8.21
1971	3.31	9.2	10.87
1972	4.97	7.2	13.14
1973	5.59	7.1	14.29
1974	6.40	9.3	13.89
1975	6.73		16.43
1976	6.90		15.46
1977	7.39		16.08
1978	7.79		16.71
1979	7.83		17.77

[1] The annual production function shifts were calculated beginning in 1956 for wheat and in 1964 for rapeseed to facilitate appropriate research lags when computing the social rates of return.

[2] Assumes a research lag of seven years.

A second aspect that is deserving of comment and justification relates to the assumption of neutrality in the production function shifts. Neutral technical change implies that the marginal products of the inputs are unchanged. In the case of new varieties, the main interest is with fertilizer inputs. If, for example, the new varieties were more responsive to fertilizer than the old varieties, then the resulting production function shifts would be biased downward to the extent of the interaction effect between varieties and fertilizers. Knott (1974, p. 1) points out for wheat that, "It is generally considered that the commercial cultivars are relatively unresponsive to fertilizer and that cultivar-fertilizer interactions do not occur." Studies by Bauer (1970) and McNeal, et al. (1971) support this view. However, other experimental studies have reported significant differences in varietal responses to fertilizer (Pittman and Tipples, 1978; Kosmolak and Crowle, 1980).

Even though the experimental evidence does not provide a clear indication of whether the marginal products of fertilizer are similar among new and old varieties of wheat and rapeseed, reliance on a few general observations implies that the differential responses are at best small. For example, the majority of the new wheat and rapeseed varieties are quite similar in genetic background to old varieties (Canadian International Grains Institute, 1975). To the extent that genetic make-up influences the plant's response to fertilizer, the differential varietal responses might be expected to be small. Additional evidence is that fertilizer recommendations do not give consideration to the variety of wheat or rapeseed being planted.

A final aspect requiring comment relates to the consideration of only yield effects. By focusing only on yield, changes in grain quality are ignored. In the case of wheat, if the new varieties have higher milling and baking quality characteristics as a result of research efforts, then the social benefits being attributed to Canadian wheat research will be biased downward. In Canada, statutory quality standards have been established for plant breeders. These standards are considered to be exceptionally high relative to those in other countries. As stated by Walton (1968, p. 601), in Canada "The objective of all hard red spring wheat breeding programs, for well over fifty years, has been to produce strains equal in quality to Marquis with added factors aimed to improve yield." This notion is supported by the overall quality ratings of the major hard red spring wheat varieties in which none of the new varieties were rated superior to Marquis (i.e., the statutory quality standard) (Canadian International Grains Institute, 1975). This implies that quality improvements in wheat have been small and, consequently, can be left out of the analysis without causing significant bias.

In the case of rapeseed, improvements in the quality and nutritional aspects of both the oil for human consumption and the meal for livestock feed are generally recognized. Oil quality was improved with the development of low erucic acid rapeseed (LEAR) varieties, and the meal was improved with the development of low glucosinolate varieties and more recently with the development of low fibre content varieties. During the period that the study covered, the improved meal quality was considered to have had a limited effect because the developments occurred near the end of the study period and because it was unknown whether the new varieties would become widely adopted by producers.

The benefits from improvements in the quality of rapeseed oil were also not included in the reported analysis. This is because, at the time of the study, little was known about the health hazards associated with the high erucic acid varieties nor what the possible impacts on the Canadian rapeseed industry might be. Consequently, only the benefits from yield improvement were considered.

Aggregate Production Function Shifts Attributable to all Public Wheat Research in Canada

The approach utilized to estimate the shifts in the aggregate wheat production function attributable to all public wheat research activities involved the specification of a supply function with sufficient flexibility that social or unconventional inputs such as research or extension expenditures could be included as variables. The contributions of public wheat research and/or extension could then be measured directly by the relative shifts in the aggregate supply function.

This approach was a logical extension of American studies that have employed production function estimates to measure the social benefits of agricultural research in which research and/or extension were included as integral variables (Peterson, 1967; Bredahl and Peterson, 1976; Davis, 1979). The rationale underlying these studies follows naturally from the view that research and extension produce and transmit new knowledge — an intermediate product or input in the agricultural production processes. The new knowledge facilitates quality improvements in conventional inputs. Hence, instead of adjusting the conventional inputs for quality change, research and extension are included as explicit variables in the production function for agricultural output.

The aggregate supply of wheat in western Canada was postulated to be a function of its own price, the price of competing products, the price of inputs, climatic factors, government programs, and public wheat research and extension expenditures. In its most general form, the supply function can be stated as:

$$Q_t = f(PW_t^*, PB_t^*, FP_t, LP_t, WS_t, DL_t, MY_t, JU_t, JY_t, PE_t, EX_t, RS_t)$$

where Q_t = quantity of wheat produced,

PW_t^* = expected farm price of wheat,

PB_t^* = expected farm price of barley,

FP_t = price of fertilizer,

LP_t = price of labour,

WS_t = quantity of wheat in storage on farms,

DL_t = dummy variable to represent federal government's LIFT program,

MY_t = precipitation received in the month of May,

JU_t = precipitation received in the month of June,

JY_t = precipitation received in the month of July,

PE_t = potential evapotranspiration in the months of June and July,

EX_t = public expenditures on wheat extension activities applicable in year t, and

RS_t = public expenditures on all wheat research activities applicable in year t.

Pooled time series-cross section data were used to estimate the constant elasticity wheat supply function (Table 3). All of the estimated parameters had signs that agreed with a priori theoretical expectations (i.e., based on economic and agronomic theory). With the exception of May rainfall and wheat extension expenditures, all parameters were statistically significant at the 95 percent level of confidence or higher. The estimated parameters for public wheat research expenditures were quite similar under various research lag assumptions. The results suggest that a 1 percent increase in the level of wheat research expenditures in year t-P, will cause wheat production in year t to increase by about 0.8 to 0.9 percent.

TABLE 3

ESTIMATED PARAMETERS FOR THE CANADIAN WHEAT SUPPLY FUNCTION UNDER THREE RESEARCH LAG ASSUMPTIONS[1]

Exogenous variables	Six-year lag	Seven-year lag	Eight-year lag
Wheat Price	1.3050*	1.3549*	1.0492*
	(3.36)	(3.40)	(2.55)
Barley Price	-1.8801*	-1.8826*	-1.5174*
	(-4.80)	(-4.61)	(-3.53)
Fertilizer Price	-0.8456*	-0.8360*	-0.8321*
	(-6.14)	(-6.02)	(-6.11)
Labour Price	-1.1832*	-1.0539*	-1.3207*
	(-4.38)	(-3.85)	(-4.80)
Farm Stocks	-0.2894*	-0.2735*	-0.2218*
	(-7.73)	(-7.46)	(-5.47)
LIFT — Dummy Variable	-0.7614*	-0.7470*	-0.7409*
	(-7.95)	(-7.35)	(-7.70)
May Rainfall	0.0183	0.0162	0.0139
	(0.80)	(0.69)	(0.58)
June Rainfall	0.3001*	0.3001*	0.3122*
	(4.15)	(4.13)	(4.31)
July Rainfall	0.1444*	0.1487*	0.1584*
	(2.05)	(2.10)	(2.14)
June-July Potential Evapotranspiration	-0.7022*	-0.7183*	-0.7362*
	(-2.55)	(-2.59)	(-2.67)
Wheat Extension Expenditures	0.0167	0.0140	0.0155
	(0.55)	(0.46)	(0.61)
Wheat Research Expenditures — 6-year lag	0.7753*		
	(2.19)		
Wheat Research Expenditures — 7-year lag		0.8998*	
		(3.22)	
Wheat Research Expenditures — 8-year lag			0.8948*
			(2.84)
R-Square	.761	.760.	762

[1] The estimated parameters for the regional intercepts (i.e., the crop districts) are not shown. The figures in brackets are the t-statistics.

* indicates significance at the 95% level of confidence or higher.

The annual shifts in the aggregate wheat supply function, attributable solely to public wheat research, were calculated under *ceteris paribus* assumptions (i.e., holding all input and product prices, weather, etc., constant) (Table 2)[8]. The formula for the relative shift (h_t) is given by:

$$h_t = \frac{Q_t - Q_b}{Q_t} = \frac{R_{t-\varrho}^{\alpha} - R_{6b}^{\alpha}}{R_{t-\varrho}^{\alpha}}$$

where Q_t = level of wheat output that comes forth in year t as a result of utilizing the new wheat technologies developed by public research,

Q_b = level of wheat output that would come forth, *ceteris paribus*, had no research been undertaken to develop new wheat technologies,

$R_{t-\varrho}$ = appropriately lagged public wheat research expenditures applicable in year t,

R_b = level of public wheat research expenditures applicable in some base year (i.e., b = t_o - -1 where t_o represents the first year for which the social benefits are being calculated, and α is the assumed research lag),

α = estimated coefficient on the wheat research variable.

RESULTS AND DISCUSSION

THE LEVEL OF SOCIAL BENEFITS

The level of social benefits (i.e., the change in consumers' plus producers' surpluses) attributable to public investment in wheat breeding and all wheat research was calculated for the period 1956-1979; that for rapeseed breeding research was calculated for the period 1964-65 to 1974-75 (Table 4). The results showed that society has benefited substantially from public investment in wheat and rapeseed research. The annual social benefits for the wheat breeding research scenario averaged $43 million (measured in 1971 dollars) and ranged from $2 million in 1960 to $141 million in 1979. For the all-wheat research scenario, the annual social benefits averaged $143 million and ranged from $23 to $362 million in the years 1956 and 1973, respectively.

The high annual variation in the level of social benefits from public wheat research activities was attributable to changes in weather and marketing opportunities for wheat and other grains. Furthermore, the levels of social benefits were relatively low in the decade beginning in 1960 compared to those in the following decade. Three possible explanations were suggested as contributing to this pattern. First, the general climatic or environmental conditions may have changed over the period of the study which, in turn, affected the relative performance of the new wheat technologies (e.g., less rainfall in the 1960s versus the 1970s, or less favourable growing conditions in the 1960s leading to increased problems

TABLE 4

ESTIMATES OF SOCIAL BENEFITS FROM PUBLIC WHEAT AND RAPESEED RESEARCH

Year	Wheat Breeding Research	All Wheat Research	Rapeseed Breeding Research
	--------(millions of 1971 dollars)--------		(millions of 1961 dollars)
1956	15.99	22.62	
1957	24.94	49.12	
1958	22.44	49.25	
1959	19.33	64.73	
1960	2.15	79.07	
1961	3.53	104.21	
1962	8.21	97.34	
1963	15.14	144.62	
1964	9.86	101.24	0.20
1965	12.37	127.04	0.66
1966	15.09	90.63	1.91
1967	21.00	56.15	1.87
1968	21.95	44.57	2.26
1969	26.65	56.71	6.08
1970	29.61	74.75	12.19
1971	30.51	104.07	10.17
1972	68.46	187.53	13.84
1973	136.57	360.83	17.70
1974	124.59	277.96	19.71
1975	116.23	294.02	
1976	92.33	214.25	
1977	106.24	239.65	
1978	117.37	259.69	
1979	140.85	328.95	

with disease and insect pests). The second explanation was that the research discovery process applicable to the 1960s did not produce much in terms of higher yielding varieties or improved wheat production practices. Consequently, producers had few new technologies to adopt.[9] The third and most plausible explanation was that producers lacked adequate economic incentives for wheat production and for the rapid adoption of new production technologies. Throughout the 1960s huge stockpiles of wheat were accumulating on farms (e.g., by 1970 farm wheat stocks were equivalent to two years of production) reflecting the lack of marketing opportunities and generally depressed prices for wheat. In the early 1970s, this trend was reversed as world demand for Canadian wheat suddenly increased causing prices to rise to unprecedented levels. The high prices and good marketing opportunities, in turn, made new wheat technologies (and complementary inputs such as fertilizers, herbicides and insecticides) economically attractive for producers to adopt.

The annual level of social benefits attributable to public investment in rapeseed breeding research averaged $7.5 million (measured in 1961 dollar values) and displayed an almost continuous upward trend. The rapid growth in the level of social benefits from rapeseed breeding research is reflective, in a large part, of the increased area being planted to this new type of crop.

The levels of social benefits from the wheat and rapeseed research activities were quite sensitive to changes in the magnitude of the production function shifts, but rather insensitive to changes in the assumptions about the supply and demand elasticities (data not shown).

SOCIAL RATES OF RETURN

Because agricultural research is an investment activity in which social benefits and costs are received and incurred over a period of time (and with a time lag), valid comparisons of the benefits and costs must be made by computing social rates of return. One of the most appealing methods of expressing the relationship between the social benefits and costs is the internal rate of return. It is defined as the rate of interest that makes the discounted benefits equal to the discounted costs at a given point in time.[10] It refers to the compound rate of interest that the investment is actually earning and has the advantage of not relying on an external opportunity cost for investment funds.

Average internal rates of return were computed for research lag assumptions (i.e., the time period before a research investment produces any social benefit) of ten, seven and four years for the wheat breeding, all-wheat and rapeseed breeding research scenarios, respectively. The annual level of future social benefits and social costs for the two wheat scenarios were assumed to equal the respective averages for the three-year period 1977-79. Furthermore, two measures of social costs were used — one that included wheat research expenditures only, and one that included wheat research and extension expenditures.[11] For rapeseed breeding research, the annual level of future social benefits was set equal to the 1972-73 level, and the annual level of future social costs was set at 35 percent of the 1974-75 research expenditure level. Furthermore, all future social benefits and costs associated with the rapeseed scenario were assumed to end arbitrarily in 1995.

The results showed that the average internal social rates of return from public investment in wheat and rapeseed research were indeed high (Table 5). The results imply that each dollar invested in wheat research produced an average annual return above the rate of inflation of 30 to 39 percent (or $0.30 to $0.39 annually) from the date of initial investment. The rate of return from public investment in rapeseed breeding research was even higher than that earned from investment in wheat research. These rates of return are much higher than those realized on most ordinary business investments and from those realized on most other types of public investments (Krutilla, 1960; Reuber and Wonnacott, 1960). The rates of return from these studies compare favourably with those reported in studies from other countries (Ruttan, 1982).

TABLE 5

AVERAGE INTERNAL RATES OF RETURN(%)
TO CANADIAN PUBLIC INVESTMENT IN WHEAT
AND RAPESEED RESEARCH

Research Scenario	Measure of social cost	
	Research Expenditures	Research & Extension Expenditures
Wheat Breeding	34	30
All-Wheat	39	34
Rapeseed Breeding	101	-

A rough or first approximation of the *marginal* social internal rates of return were also made for the wheat research scenarios.[12] For the wheat breeding scenario, the marginal internal rate of return was 44 percent when research expenditures were used as the measure of social costs. This implies that the last dollar invested in wheat breeding research produced an annual return of 44 percent or, in an *ex ante* sense, it implies that an additional dollar invested in wheat breeding research will produce an annual return of about 44 percent. Similarly, for the all-wheat research scenario, the marginal internal rate of return was 59 percent.

DISTRIBUTION OF THE SOCIAL BENEFITS

Because of the public good nature of the output from agricultural research, public support is considered necessary in order to attain a socially optimum level of investment. However, if the major share of the social benefits from public research are captured by one group or another, then it might be more appropriate, in terms of equity criteria, to let the groups share in the investment costs in proportion to the benefits received.

The methodological framework used in these studies provides a means for estimating the proportion of the total social benefits going to producers and non-producers (i.e., consumers), respectively. Unfortunately, such analysis has several limitations. First, the theoretical framework is only a partial equilibrium approach and, consequently, it ignores all second-order effects. Second, it ignores many of the equity and interpersonal utility comparison issues for members within and between groups (e.g., do large producers benefit relatively more or less than small producers; how are the social benefits distributed between low and high income consumers; etc.?).[13] Finally, it ignores the fact that agricultural producers are, at the same time, consumers.

With these considerations in mind, the results of this analysis showed that producers and consumers shared in the social benefits of public wheat and rapeseed research. For the wheat breeding research scenario, wheat producers received an average of 62 percent of the total social benefits, while consumers received the remaining 38 percent. Similarly, for the all-wheat research scenario, producers received an average of 65 percent and consumers 35 percent of the total social benefits. Finally, for the rapeseed breeding research scenario, producers received 47 percent and consumers 53 percent.

The social benefits received by producers will be divided among the factors of production in inverse proportion to their elasticity of supply. Since the supply of land is highly inelastic in nature, land owners receive a proportionately large share of the benefits going to producers in the form of an increased rent to land. The increased economic rent, in turn, becomes capitalized into the price of farm land (Dyck, 1979).

Similarly, since a large share of the annual wheat and rapeseed production is exported, a sizeable share of the social benefits going to consumers is actually passed along to foreign countries. This transfer takes the form of larger quantities of wheat and rapeseed products being made available at lower prices. However, Canadian consumers (and producers) benefit indirectly, at least to the same extent. The foreign exchange earnings from the additional exports enable Canadians to purchase foreign goods and services at lower prices.

The distribution of the social benefits between producers and consumers was extremely sensitive to changes in the demand and supply elasticity assumptions (data not shown). In general, the lower the demand elasticity values, and the higher the supply elasticity values, the greater was the proportion of the total annual social benefits captured by consumers as a group. Similarly, the higher the demand elasticity values, and the lower the supply elasticity values, the greater was the proportion of the benefits captured by producers as a group.

SUMMARY AND CONCLUDING COMMENTS

The responsibility for funding agricultural research activities in Canada falls largely upon governments because of the structure of the industry and the nature of the research output. In recent years, society has questioned the value of these public investments and the efficiency with which the resources are being allocated. This report has attempted to provide some information on these aspects as they relate to wheat and rapeseed research activities.

The results of the empirical studies examined provide documented evidence to the question of whether society has benefited from public investment in agricultural research. The answer must be an unequivocal YES. The level of social benefits and social rates of return from investment in wheat and rapeseed research (i.e., in the range of 30 to 101 percent annually) are generally much higher than the 10 to 20 percent rate of return expected on most ordinary business investments and from those realized on most other types of public investment opportunities. The high marginal rates of return imply that society may be underinvesting in agricultural research (i.e., the marginal social benefits from investment in agricultural research are substantially above the opportunity costs of investments funds). Consequently, increased funding for agricultural research should be a key element in all future agri-food, regional development and national development strategies in Canada.

NOTES

1. In practice, one generally finds private firms undertaking agricultural research activities only in those areas where the output can be easily embodied in some physical input or intermediate product (e.g., farm machinery, buildings, pesticides). For these types of research activities, well-defined markets exist for the sale of the research output. The research resource allocation and investment decisions are made primarily through the market place. The price mechanism performs the dual role of allocating research resources and distributing the rewards. As a result, the research priorities followed by private firms are determined largely by the relative expected prices and costs (i.e., expected profitability).

2. Annual cost estimates (both variable and overhead) were made because of changes in the real costs of conducting research. The techniques of experimentation and investigation have become more complex and sophisticated over the years (as have the problems themselves) and the research equipment and necessary resources have become correspondingly more expensive. On the other hand, new equipment (e.g., computers) has been installed, primarily to reduce the amount of time and resources utilized in collecting and processing data.

3. An index of associate professors' salaries was used to deflate the wheat research and extension expenditures to real dollars instead of the commonly used Consumer Price Index (CPI) because professional salaries, which weigh heavily in the cost of supporting a scientist, have risen substantially faster than the CPI over the past thirty years. Consequently, using the CPI underestimates past research and extension expenditures relative to those in current time periods.

4. The theoretically correct measurement of consumers' surplus is the area below the Hicks compensated demand function and above the price line. In empirical applications the area below the ordinary or Marshallian demand curve is used. Little bias is introduced into the measurement if the income elasticity of demand for the product is small or if the product represents a small portion of the total budget expenditures of consumers. For most agricultural products, both of these conditions normally apply (see Hassan and Johnson, 1976).

5. Formulas to approximate the various areas are given in Hayami and Akino (1977).

6. Because of space limitations, only the latter aspect is discussed in some detail in this paper. Readers interested in the details of the other aspects can consult Zentner (1982), and Nagy and Furtan (1978).

7. The (simplified) formula used for calculating the annual shifts in the aggregate wheat and rapeseed production functions (K_t) was:

$$K_t = \underset{ij}{\Sigma\Sigma} \left[\frac{Y_{ijt} - Y_{bjt}}{Y_{ijt}} \right] \frac{A_{ijt}}{A_t}$$

where i   = variety of wheat or rapeseed (i = 1,2,...,I),
       j   = geographical region (j = 1,2,...,J),
       t   = time period or year (t = 1,2,...,T),
       Y_{ijt} = average yield of variety i in region j and period t,
       Y_{bjt} = average yield of base variety b in region i and period t,
       A_{ijt} = area sown to variety i in region j and period t, and
       A_t = total area sown to wheat or rapeseed in period t.

8. The annual shifts in the aggregate wheat supply function were transformed into shifts in the aggregate wheat production function (for comparative purposes) by dividing by the constant $(1+\varepsilon)$ where the price elasticity of supply, $\varepsilon = 1.2364$. This follows from the relationship that $h_t \approx (1+\varepsilon)K_t$.

9. One example may have been the diversion of Canadian wheat breeders to the development of true hybrid wheat varieties. This effort was unsuccessful and has since been discontinued.

10. The expression for the internal rate of return is given by the formula:

$$\sum_{t=0}^{T} \frac{C_t}{(1+r_i)^t} = \sum_{t=0}^{T} \frac{B_t}{(1+r_i)^t}$$

where r_i = internal rate of interest,
       C_t = social costs in year t,
       B_t = social benefits in year t, and
       T   = year in which the research ceases to produce benefits.

The internal rate of return is interpreted to mean that on average each dollar invested in agricultural research returned r_i percent annually above the rate of inflation from the date of initial investment.

11. This approach was followed because of the statistical insignificance of the estimated parameter for the wheat extension variable, and the view held by some economists that research and extension are intricately related.

12. Marginal internal rates of return are important in public research resource allocation decisions. For a given research expenditure, research resources are allocated efficiently when the marginal internal rates of return are equated across all possible research projects.

13. With respect to this latter example, it is known *a priori* that low income consumers benefit relatively more from new agricultural technologies than high income consumers. This occurs because low income consumers spend proportionately more of their disposable income on food items.

REFERENCES

Bauer, A. "Effect of Fertilizer Nitrogen Rate on Yield of Six Spring Wheats." *Canadian Journal of Plant Science* 54 (1974): 1-7.

Bredahl, M.E., and W. Peterson. "The Productivity and Allocation of Research: U.S. Agricultural Experiment Stations." *American Journal of Agricultural Economics* 58 (1976): 684-692.

Canadian International Grains Institute. *Grains and Oilseeds: Handling, Marketing and Processing.* Winnipeg, Manitoba: Canadian International Grains Institute, 1975.

Davis, J.S. "Stability of the Research Production Function Coefficient for U.S. Agriculture." Ph.D. diss., University of Minnesota, St. Paul, Minnesota, 1979.

Dyck, J.D. "The Impact of Adopted Technological Change on Farmland Prices in Manitoba." M.Sc. Thesis, University of Manitoba, Winnipeg, Manitoba, 1979.

Hassan, Z.A., and S.R. Johnson. "Consumer Demand for Major Foods in Canada." Ottawa, Canada: Agriculture Canada, Economic Branch Publication 76/2, 1976.

Hayami, Y., and M. Akino. "Organization and Productivity of Agricultural Research Systems in Japan." In *Resource Allocation and Productivity*, edited by T.M. Arndt, D.G. Dalrymple, and V.W. Ruttan. Minneapolis, Minnesota: University of Minnesota Press, 1977.

Kaldor, D.R. "Social Returns to Research and the Objectives of Public Research." In *Resource Allocation in Agricultural Research*, edited by W.L. Fishel. Minneapolis, Minnesota: University of Minnesota Press, 1971.

Kislev, Y., and W. Peterson. "Induced Innovations and Farm Mechanization." *American Journal of Agricultural Economics* 63 (1981): 562-565.

Knott, D.R. "Effects of Nitrogen Fertilizer on the Yield and Protein Content of Five Spring Wheats." *Canadian Journal of Plant Science* 54 (1974): 1-7.

Kosmolak, F.G., and W.L. Crowle. "An Effect of Nitrogen Fertilization on the Agronomic Traits and Dough Mixing Strengths of Five Canadian Hard Red Spring Wheat Cultivars." *Canadian Journal of Plant Science* 60 (1980): 1071-1076.

Krutilla, J.V. *Sequence and Timing in River Basin Development: With Special Applications to Canadian-United States Columbia River Basin Planning.* Resources for the Future, Inc., February 1960.

McLaughlin, G.R. "A Study Regarding Agricultural Research in Canada." Regina, Saskatchewan: Research Division, Saskatchewan Wheat Pool, 1977.

McNeal, F.H., M.A. Berg, P.L. Brown, and C.F. McGuire. "Productivity and Quality Response of Five Spring Wheat Genotypes, *Triticum aestivum* L., to Nitrogen Fertilizer." *Agronomy Journal* 63 (1971): 908-910.

Nagy, J.G., and W.H. Furtan. "Economic Costs and Returns from Crop Development Research: The Case of Rapeseed Breeding in Canada." *Canadian Journal of Agricultural Economics* 26 (1978): 1-14.

Peterson, W.L. "Return to Poultry Research in the United States." *Journal of Farm Economics* 49 (1967): 565-569.

Pittman, U.J., and K.H. Tipples. "Survival, Yield, Protein Content and Baking Quality of Hard Red Winter Wheats Grown under Various Fertilizer Practices in Southern Alberta." *Canadian Journal of Plant Science* 58 (1978): 1049-1060.

Reuber, G.L., and R.J. Wonnacott. *The Cost of Social Capital in Canada: With Special Reference to Public Development of the Columbia River.* London, Ontario: University of Western Ontario, January 1960.

Ruttan, V.W. *Agricultural Research Policy.* Minneapolis, Minnesota: University of Minnesota Press, 1982.

Walton, P.D. "Spring Wheat Variety Trials in the Prairie Provinces." *Canadian Journal of Plant Science* 48 (1968): 601-609.

Zentner, R.P. "An Economic Evaluation of Public Wheat Research Expenditures in Canada." Ph.D. diss., University of Minnesota, St. Paul, Minnesota, 1982.